The Flight of the Albatross

Voyages with my Father, the Unsung Hero

Margrethe Alexandroni

The Flight of the Albatross

Margrethe Alexandroni

Paperback Edition First Published in Great Britain
in 2015 by aSys Publishing

eBook Edition First Published in Great Britain
in 2015 by aSys Publishing

ISBN: 978-1-910757-23-9
aSys Publishing
http://www.asys-publishing.co.uk

Contents

Preface

At the beginning of World War II the Norwegian Merchant fleet was the fourth largest in the world. *The Norwegian Shipping and Trade Mission (Nortraship)* was established in London in April 1940 to administer the Norwegian merchant fleet outside German-controlled areas. Nortraship operated some 1,000 vessels and was the largest shipping company in the world. According to Sir Winston Churchill the sailors of the Norwegian merchant fleet were worth more than a million soldiers. The fact is that without the Norwegian tankers the British would not have had the aviation fuel to put the Hawker Hurricanes and Spitfires into the sky and the Allies would have lost the war. When the German Wehrmacht occupied Norway on April 9th 1940 the Norwegian traitor and Nazi puppet, Vidkun Quisling, sent out an edict to the captain of every Norwegian ship in foreign waters to sail to German, Italian or neutral ports and join the German war effort. The captains of the Norwgian ships followed King Haakon's command from exile, ignored the order, joined Nortraship and sailed under Allied command instead.

694 Norwegian ships were sunk during the war years representing 47% of the total fleet. More than 3,700 Norwegian merchant seamen lost their lives. A sizeable percentage seeing that in 1940 the entire population of Norway only counted about 3million people.

From this valiant contribution grew a scandal that is a source of bitterness till this very day.

This is what happened: In 1940 the Norwegian sailors were paid more than their British counterparts, mainly due to higher war hazard pay. The British government worried that this would have an adverse effect on British sailors and pressed for a wage reduction. It was agreed that the wage difference should be placed in a special fund, which became known as Nortraship's Secret Fund, secret because the British sailors were not to know about it, to be paid to the Norwegian sailors after the war. The sailors accepted this in good faith, believing that after the war there would be a nest egg waiting for them. This was not to be. Instead the government and seamen's organisations suggested that the money be distributed as assistance to needy seamen and seamen's widows. Thus the seamen's organisations went against their own members. A lengthy legal process ensued which the government won in the Norwegian Supreme Court in 1954. It created much bitterness among the sailors who felt cheated out of what was rightfully theirs. The struggle continued for many years and was never resolved to the seamen's satisfaction.

Throughout the war my father, Kristoffer Hoddevik, was the captain of oil tankers sailing in convoys in the world's most dangerous waters under threat from German planes, warships and submarines. To me, born after the war, these years were like a closed chapter of which he spoke very little. It was only after I started researching this period that I learnt the facts behind the convoys and got some idea of what it must have been like. And, how the Norwegian sailors received little or no recognition for their bravery and sacrifice.

Growing up in social democratic post war Norway I was aware of this dark and arduous time in my father's life that set us apart and made us stand out and be different in a society that placed great emphasis on sameness – that everybody should be as alike as possible.

This then, is the story of a boy growing up in a small fishing/farming community in Western Norway who became the captain of a giant oil tanker sailing in convoys in perilous waters. It's the story of the house he planned to build if he made it through the war, a unique and magical house that is a focal point for his descendants. It's my own story of growing up in social democratic Norway during the 1950s and 60s when being different was viewed with suspicion, ridicule and hostility. It is the story of the war-sailors' anger and bitterness for being cast aside and ignored rather than celebrated for their courage and contribution to the Allied war effort. It's the story of the pettiness and envy meted out to us as a family for having a house slightly bigger than our neighbours. And, it is the story of my own travels in my father's footsteps to places like Rio, Buenos Aires, China and Namibia, Liverpool and Greenock and of how, more than thirty years after his passing, I am now closer to him than I ever was in his lifetime.

The Skeleton Coast, Namibia 2011

A day so wonderful.

When the ancient mariners got shipwrecked off the coast of South-West Africa they sometimes managed to swim or float to the shore only to be met by an awesome sight: Sand and nothing but sand as far as the eye could see, and much further still. Nothing to eat or drink and nowhere to go. The only thing the mariner could do was to sit down and wait for somebody to come by and save him, but who could that be, on this desolate shore with nothing but endless sea and miles and miles of desert. And so, waiting and hoping, he fell asleep never to wake up. His bones were soon picked clean by jackals and sea gulls, white and dry they remained on the beach like whispering headstones giving the long coastline of Namibia its name.

Today I stood on that shore. For a long time I was watching the awesome waves form, rise and crash against the sand, peter out, and be gone.

I walked along the shore by myself. There was no danger from marauding pickpockets. All along the seafront are villas and guest houses, people out walking. One girl stood for ages photographing the surf. Enormous seashells lay on the ground, mostly mussels as big as your hand. I picked up the biggest and cleanest ones hoping to take them back to England. The beach stretches on and on, but I couldn't keep walking forever. Soon the short tropical dusk would descend, change into night and it would be too dark to see where I was.

When I turned to walk back there was a perfect rainbow in the fog, its colours muted like all the other colours along this fantastical coastline.

I had read about the fog that forms when the cold South-Atlantic meets the hot sands of the desert. Nobody told me that the fog was this cold, like droplets of icy rain. Everything that lives here draws its life from the fog. Tiny plants with hard thick leaves drink from it. Beetles sit on the leaves, their lower parts in the air; fog condenses on their backs and trickles down into their mouths. The beetles become food for lizards, snakes and birds.

* * *

Earlier today, on a sea safari starting from Walvis Bay, down the coast from Swakopmund where my son, Samy, and I are staying, I saw two hump-backed whales, their backs like mounds above the waterline. Seals came onto our boat, three different ones, one after the other. Tony, the captain cum guide told us that the seals always recognise his boat amongst all the others. The seals were all males, a solid mass of muscle and blubber. Beautiful dark-brown eyes, slick and cold to the touch, and all black.

We were far from the only boat out this morning. There were other sight-seeing boats like ours, and some weird contraptions that looked like cages on water, or some kind of tiny primitive oil rigs. Tony said they were for fishing shrimps. Further out were bigger ships, which set me thinking about my father, the ship's captain, the war hero. All through the Second World War he was captaining an oil tanker, transporting oil for the Allies.

Sitting on the deck of a peaceful tourist boat I couldn't stop thinking about all the times my father must have sailed by this exact strip of coast, further out of course, too far to observe any wildlife, except for whales and dolphins, but close enough to see the strip of desert land and for all I know, the lights of the shrimp boats fishing at night. There was nothing he loved more than rounding the craggy coast of the Cape of Good Hope with the albatrosses circling above. Flying with the albatross around the Cape, as he expressed it. Once he sent me a black and white photo that he had taken of an albatross directly above his ship, telling me about its 12 foot wingspan. All you saw was the one bird silhouetted against the sky, nothing else on the photo to illustrate the sheer size of it. I was only nine or ten years old and had never heard about an albatross, so the photo didn't mean much to me. It would have meant a lot now, but sadly it's been lost.

It is cold, like winter in England. Wearing a jumper and an anorak you're warm enough during the day, but as soon as the daylight starts to fade, the damp and cold creep into your bones.

After my walk along the seafront I went up into the lounge of the guest house. More like a private sitting room with deep chairs and an open fire place. The receptionist had baked a batch of cupcakes with salted caramel topping, one Namibian dollar each. I bought one and she made me a cup of coffee. I could easily have managed another muffin but didn't want to appear too greedy. She had also lit a fire, very homely and cosy. I was sitting writing my journal when Samy came and joined me. He had ordered a taxi and it was time go into Swakopmund proper for dinner.

Life is full of hope and we must never give up hoping, not even when our lives are at a stand-still and we feel imprisoned behind grey walls. A hole in the wall will open and we'll fly like the albatross, gliding on outstretched wings above the sea. Ever since I first heard about the Skeleton Coast of Namibia I was hoping one day to set foot there, and today I have.

Norway,
January 2000

Soon after New Year 2000, January 8 to be precise, I arranged a big party in my parents' house. Sam and I had flown in two days previously.

It was dark when we arrived in the early evening. The house standing tall on top of a hill, the way it has stood for longer than I remember. John dropped us off at the bottom of the drive. He was on night duty at Oslo Airport where he worked and couldn't come up with us. The snow was ankle deep. Nobody had cleared a passage. There were footprints, presumably John's. We placed our feet in the footprints and lumbered up the hill, lugging our cases. It was years since I'd last been to Norway at this time of year. The air was icy and so clean you could drink it, no sound except for the faint hum of the forest. The kitchen was lit. For a fleeting moment I thought I saw Mum's white-haired head in the window, looking out as she always did when expecting me home. But no, she wasn't there, and the kitchen was the only room with the light on. The outside lamp was on too, making it easy to unlock the front door. But there the illusion ended. When we entered the house it felt cold and dank, its soul dead or asleep.

Apart from that everything was as it had always been: The tall mirror in the hallway placed opposite the door so the first thing you saw upon entering was your own image looking back at you . . . Mum's hats and scarves on the shelf and her coats and jackets in the wardrobe below, the little telephone table by the mirror, the solid wooden chair next to it that John once weed on when he was sleepwalking thinking it was the toilet. He was eight at the time. In the morning he remembered nothing about it and I had to swear never to tell him. The paintings on the living room walls...

4

The furniture I had grown up with stood where it had always stood—the sideboard in the dining room with the hand-carved wooden candleholder with five half-burnt pink candles and in front of it the ship in a bottle that a sailor had once made for my father, a clumsy looking thing, but Dad had always insisted on giving it pride of place in his home and Mum had kept it that way even after he'd gone. The calendar on the kitchen wall still on September, the month Mum moved into the nursing home. All the lamps worked. Here and there odds and ends that had never been tidied away, a red woolly blanket thrown across an armchair, a reel of cotton, an opened letter from my auntie Astrid on the dining table and a couple of magazines—as if Mum had popped out for something and would be back in a moment. Cutlery, crockery, glasses, coffee, tea, sugar, flour, washing-up liquid . . . everything was as she left it.

I had rung John from London asking him to turn on the heating and leave us some survival rations till we could get to the shops, specifically mentioning coffee, bread, milk, eggs and cheese. Which was exactly what he had brought, minus coffee as there was already some in the house.

John may have turned on the heating but still the house felt cold and desolate. The chill had crept into its bones, and it would take days to drive it away. There were dead flies on the window sills, and the pot-plants were beyond saving. Dead ants with white powder sprinkled on top covered a corner of the dining room floor. We'd never had ants before. Some sort of group intelligence must have told them that the house was now empty and that it would be an ideal hide-away for the winter. John had come by, spotted them and covered them in insecticide. It hadn't occurred to him to vacuum up the mess. One good thing, he had emptied the fridge, so no smell of rotting food.

Mum's move to the nursing home had never been planned. She'd been ailing for some time and her doctor had diagnosed a touch of pneumonia and arranged for her to go into the nursing home for a rest. At first she hated it, but when she was considered well enough to return home, she couldn't face sitting on her own in a large empty house waiting for a nurse who might turn up now or in three hours. And so, to our surprise, she had asked to stay permanently. John had been round to collect some of her clothes and photographs and a few ornaments. Apart from that everything remained as it was on the day she left.

Slept in fits and starts. Towards morning when I thought it would soon be time to get up, some kind of half-dream about a man and woman in black walking about outside my window, looking for a way into the house. Wrapping my duvet around me I opened the window to let them in, but then it struck me that this was stupid, letting strangers in just like that. They wanted the doctor's surgery somewhere else in the house and I pointed them in the right direction. All the time I knew exactly where I was. With the layer of sleep growing thinner I started wondering how the couple could have walked past my window looking in when my room was on the first floor. I found no answer to this question and gradually the last remnants of sleep drifted away and I turned on the light, a bolt of pleasure shooting through me; it was true, I really had woken up in Norway, back in the house where I grew up. Outside it was pitch black. The drawn-out grey light of morning still hours away.

We had left the heating on and the house was warmer, less dismal, as if slowly waking from a deep slumber. By the time I had vacuumed up the ants and dead flies and cobwebs in the corners it felt normal, back to its old self, like when it was lived in.

We didn't have much time. My older son, Adam, would be arriving in the evening, and after that the nephews would claim us, and tomorrow it would be time to think about the party. And, visit Mum of course. She wasn't expecting us till tomorrow. Sam and I had both brought wine and brandy from Heathrow and Adam would bring some booze as well. Popular on account of the inflated alcohol prices in Norway.

The long Nordic dawn had receded to reveal a grey and cloudy morning. Black trees with snow-covered branches silhouetted against the grey sky and the white surface of the frozen lake, a few snowflakes fluttering through the air. Two bullfinches in the tree by the garden gate. Mum used to feed them. Had they somehow sensed that the house was coming back to life and returned in the hope of seeds and bread-crumbs? I scattered some crumbs on the snow and immediately they were there; sparrows, yellow finches, red-breasted bull finches, and a jay with its smoky pink body and blue-striped wings.

This day was our day, no family members lavishing us with attention. Keen to make the most of it we decided to take the bus to Oslo. The snow lay on the ground and the landscape was without colour, like travelling through a black and white photograph.

Around 2pm with daylight already fading we made our way up to Akershus Castle, built in the 13th century to protect Oslo against attacks from the fjord. As we walked through one of the heavy archways, a group of the King's guardsmen came marching towards us, their boots echoing against the ancient cobble stones, a scene straight from the Middle Ages. Pressed up against the heavy stone wall we stopped to let them pass. Then we climbed to the top of the battlements taking in the view and the atmosphere. We were the only people there. The grass was covered in a layer of frosty snow, less snow here than further inland where we stayed. Below us the Oslofjord was heaving and rolling against the shore, calm and steely grey, not many boats. Across the sound lay the peninsulas of Nesodden and Bygdøy, dark and flecked with snow.

Nesodden—where I had set foot only once, it must have been in 1959, the first and only time my father's ship had anchored in Norway, at the back and beyond of Nesodden, to discharge its cargo of oil; and we had spent one night on his ship . . . Weird things—those distant memories—you don't think of them for years, but then something triggers them and up the crop like a jack in a box and you know that they have been there all along—a glowing ember adding depth to your life.

We headed for home by the 3pm bus. Both of us lost in our own thoughts and quietly contemplating the blue light of dusk in a snow covered landscape. By the time we reached Sundvollen with its little supermarket it was pitch dark.

The Party

Adam arrived not long after Sam and I got back from Oslo. More than the party he was looking forward to spending two days in Granny's and Granddad's house. We all were.

The boys and I used to stay for a month every summer except for a couple of summers when my parents visited us. We had very little money back then and every year Mum and Dad would send me money for our tickets. No sooner had the cheque cleared than I ran to the travel agent and booked our return flight to Norway. Maher only joined us twice. He didn't find the Norwegian countryside very interesting so he stayed at home, leaving us to enjoy the world of my childhood, and for me to speak my language without worrying about Maher being bored and having to translate for him. This went on until Adam was 15 and started to get restless at Granny's, so we left him with Maher. Sam never tired of Norway. He would sleep in John's old bedroom, by then dilapidated and with some of John's odds and ends still there. The room was south-facing with plenty of sunshine and there was nothing Sam loved more than to sit there and read and think.

Maher and I first brought Adam when he was eight months old. My older brother, Bjørn, was very much in the picture that summer. He only lived some 200 yards away with Randi, his wife, and their four sons, Rune, Kai, Jarle and André. We spent a lot of time by the lake. Eastern Norway is sunny and warm in summer and people while away the days sunbathing on the shore and swimming in the cool water. Besides there isn't much to do out in the countryside, so swimming is what people do. Children learn to swim from the grown-ups and older children. People bring waffles and jam or grill sausages on an open fire by the waterside. Bjørn carried Adam into the lake and dipped him in the water. He loved it and splashed around waiving his little arms and legs.

On the last evening of our visit Bjørn came walking up the drive; blue jacket, shoebox under his arm. He had bought Adam a pair of little boots. He stayed for a while having a whisky with my father, then he went back home. I stood watching him as he walked down the hill, the sound of his footsteps on the gravel growing fainter. An eerie feeling came over me that this would be the last I'd see of him. This seemed totally groundless as he had promised to come to the airport the following day to see us off; yet there it was.

So there we sat at the airport, Mum, Dad, Adam, Maher and I. Adam was growing restless. In our minds Maher and I had left already, none of us could think of much to say. We were only waiting for Bjørn. In the end we decided that he wasn't going to come, something must have prevented him, so we said our good byes and walked through security, which was when he turned up, missing us by a couple of minutes.

The next time we came to Norway Adam was nearly three, and Bjørn was no more. Too late it was discovered that the headaches, dizzy spells and high blood pressure that had been plaguing him were not caused by stress and over-work as the doctors had believed, but by a brain tumour. For three years they had been prescribing beta blockers, treating the symptoms rather than investigating the cause.

Adam had been looking forward to travelling in an aeroplane, or preferably a helicopter. I told him we'd just have to see what they sent for us, if we got a helicopter, fine; if not we'd have to make do with a plane. When it turned out to be a plane, he was excited all the same. Mum and Dad picked us up at the airport. Dad in his black beret and checked shirt and mum in a blue dress and her grey helmet of hair freshly styled. We had lunch, pork chops and frankfurters with ice cream for dessert. Afterwards Randi and Mum's sister, Auntie Johanna, dropped by and we had coffee and cakes in the garden. Johanna had married a Swede named Gustav Glad and been living in Stockholm ever since. She would spend a week or two with their brother, Karl, who lived further along the road; but I hadn't seen her for years.

Coffee over. Randi and Auntie Johanna had left, which was when Adam thought it time we made a move as well. Logical really, we'd had our lunch and coffee; time to go home. At first I didn't get his reasoning so I just said: 'No, we can't go home yet.'

'But I want to go home now.'

Finally I twigged. He had no idea that when you go away to another country it's normal to stay for a while, nor had it occurred to me to explain it. In the end I told him that the last plane had gone and we would have to stay till tomorrow. This he accepted. The following morning he must have talked to my father for he came to me very serious and said: 'Granddad thinks a few more days.' After that he settled in *the big house*, as he called it, and all was well.

And there we were again; my two boys and I like in the old days, except this time Mum was not there; and of course neither was Dad. He passed away nearly 20 year ago. Adam remembers him clearly, and somehow Sam does too, even though he was only two and a half when Dad left us.

The house had warmed up faster than I expected. Sam and I had stopped at the supermarket on our way from Oslo and bought more food, frozen pizzas like in Mum's time, and stuff for the party. The house was peaceful, everything as it had been when we were growing up, Mum wasn't one for getting rid of her solid oak furniture simply because something else had come into fashion, or to shift heavy sideboards around for the mere sake of it. New curtains now and then, yes, and a new painting or getting rid of a lamp and buying a new one . . . But all in all things remained the same.

Outside it was snowing. Most of all we wanted to stay in the house and just be, to be left in peace and take in the atmosphere. It would be our last chance. John and his wife, Åse, were set to take over the house. Plans were afoot for major changes—extending the kitchen, adding a washroom, bringing their own furniture and fittings. The house would still be there, but nothing would be the same.

However, a night of peace and pizza was not an option. As we were putting away our shopping Randi called asking us for dinner. Her second oldest son, Kai, and his family were coming too and would be picking us up in an hour's time. One hour was better than nothing, at least time for a quiet cup of tea, but no sooner had I made the tea and Adam had put his things in his bedroom than Kai was there. He is one of those people who are always early. Tardiness is bad, but earliness is worse—people turning up before you are ready for them. It wasn't that we didn't want to go to Randi's; it was simply that we would have loved to spend this precious evening in the house that had meant so much to us, now that it was warm and inviting and we had it to ourselves for what might be the last time. We couldn't see John and Åse welcoming us with open arms. With no children they were set in their ways. Having us in the house would be an imposition. When Mum lived there, visiting her had been like returning to a prolonged childhood, but nothing lasts forever.

Randi had cooked ham with mustard sauce and asparagus and baby potatoes. She had covered her sideboard in cotton wool and made a display of miniature Christmas elves and trees as she had done every Christmas since she and Bjørn got married at the age of 20, and I was eight. Another remnant of my childhood soon to disappear. Randi was only 64 but showing early signs of dementia. But today she was fine and pleased to see us.

The day of the party arrived. I had bought seven blue African violets and blue candles which I had distributed throughout the rooms; plus blue serviettes. The idea was for our guests to take home a violet as a memento of the occasion. Later people remarked how lovely it was to see all the blue after all the red of Christmas. Randi had offered to come at 3pm and make meatballs, said she was famous for her meatballs so that would be her contribution. I expected her to arrive before 3, but when it had gone 4 and she still hadn't turned up, I rang her:

'What happened? You were supposed to come and make meatballs.'

'No, I wasn't.'

'When are you coming then?'

'I'm going to visit a friend now, and then I'm coming to the party at 7.'

My heart went cold. A healthy person may forget things but will remember when reminded. This was different. Randi had no memory of our agreement at all; it was gone, disappeared without a trace. Pursuing the issue would only upset her so I said fine and decided to make the meatballs myself. The little supermarket in Sundvollen was limited, but we had managed to find what we needed, like extra lean mince, so there was no problem. After that I made scrambled eggs with cream and chives, a Norwegian speciality served cold from the fridge, to go with the smoked salmon John would be bringing. So there I was in Mum's kitchen, cooking, looking out at the snow, the smell of meatballs and fried onions spreading throughout the house.

* * *

The party was a success. Rune, Kai, Jarle and André arrived with their wives and children, six in all from the age of two to eighteen. Anne-Lise, my friend, and her 12-year old son and his best friend also came. Everybody brought something to eat or drink: cold meat, bread, cakes, fruit, salad . . . We put the food and drink in the kitchen and people helped themselves and sat where they liked. During her last years in the house Mum had shied away from inviting people; close family could pop in for coffee and waffles but that was all she could cope with. But now, the house that had been dejected and silent for so long resounded with talk and laughter. John dug out some old vinyl records with *The Bee Gees* and *The Beach Boys* that we played on the old music system we'd had since we were teenagers. Mum's curtains framing the windows, her and Dad's paintings on the walls, the photographs I'd grown up with, the furniture that hadn't been sat on for months . . . Now I wonder what a passing stranger might have made of it all—a stranger to the area who had driven past a few times and noticed the large dark house on top of the hill and wondered why it was empty. What if he happened by that precise night and saw yellow light emanating from its windows and heard music and party sounds wafting across the fields. But then, when he next passed by the house would be as dark and silent as ever. Would he imagine that the ghosts of inhabitants past had been having a ball, or would he think that the lights, the voices and music had been figments of his imagination?

There were parties in my parents' time too. Birthdays were duly celebrated. Above all I remember winter Sundays when Auntie Entse and Uncle Arne and Dad's unmarried sister, Auntie Astrid, came to visit. They often brought red tulips. This was before every shop and petrol station sold imported flowers from Kenya all year round. You had to wait for the first tulips to be in season, which happened in late February—early March, flown in from Holland when Norway was still knee-deep in snow. At night Mum put the tulips out in the cool hallway to prolong their life. I could study them for ages . . . their faint sweet smell . . . their pale-green leaves and stems that squeaked when you touched them.

The parties of old were different though, for starters we were all much younger, Mum and Dad still going strong. Mum would have us all sitting around an extended dining table, beautifully laid with flowers of the season and candles in the silver candlesticks that she would have polished for the occasion. Kids sitting at a smaller table by themselves. Drinks would be controlled, offered around nicely and politely. This party was livelier, almost raucous, with everybody milling around, sitting where they pleased and helping themselves to food and drink.

Then again some things remained the same. At one stage the nephews' wives and I were in the kitchen rinsing plates and sorting out cakes and I thought how lovely it was, a new generation partying in the house, standing by the sink where mum and the aunties had stood. The house smiled and laughed and held us in a loving embrace. Little did it know that it was to be the last party it would see for a long time.

Two days later it was time to return to England. Cold, dull day. Grey sky. The snow on top of the frozen lake had turned to ice, the same colour as the sky. The white trunks of giant silver birches silhouetted against a forest so dark green it was nearly black. Blue-tits, yellow finches, red-breasted bullfinches and sparrows were feasting on bread left over from the party. In a couple of hours we'd be gone and no more crumbs on the snow. The place was so quiet. Apart from the birds there was no life at all, except for the odd car driving by on the road. My father hated the Norwegian winter, hated the snow, said it was like the hand of death. He often spoke of the oppressive heat in the Persian Gulf, but never said that he hated it. He told us of a flock of birds he had seen when sailing through the Panama Canal. Some were blue, some were red and some were white. The fantastic thing was that the white birds were so brilliantly white, the red ones so bright red, and the blue ones so fantastically blue. Perhaps I'll get to see them one day.

After the party the house grew silent. John and Åse didn't want parties, too much hassle and too expensive. It was no use telling them that the party the boys and I had arranged actually cost us very little. Åse's latest glass purchases and piles of home furnishing magazines fill up the tables. She loves visiting the ancient glass factory further up country, as do I, so we often go there together, a beautiful place by a lake with an indoor and outdoor cafeteria. The artistic glassware is wonderful but too expensive and heavy for me to take to England. My parents' furniture has been replaced with a mixture of modern things and genuine antiques. Rotting window frames have been substituted. A new porch has been built, the kitchen extended and a washroom added for the washing machine and dryer, other than that the rooms are the same. John spends a lot of time in front of his flat screen or listening to jazz and 60s and 70s music like Jonny Cash, which I like as well. There is Timo, their ginger chow-chow, who basically runs the household.

"I thought I'd always be full of people, but I'm quite happy really," it said to me when Åse and John weren't listening, "there is warmth in my walls and light from my windows, and that's the main thing."

Midwinter, view from the house, all white and quiet. A landscape totally void of colour. (Photo, Åse Ruud)

The Chinese Mugs

I was back in Norway in the house where I grew up. Lots of people about. One of my sons, not sure which one, was getting married that day. I had bought a beautiful outfit for the occasion, pink skirt just below the knees and a sheer sleeveless top with a pattern of large, mainly pink flowers. Pink shoes the same colour as the skirt. Two pairs of tights with pink stripes hanging to dry in the garden shed, they were not new and plain tights might have looked more sophisticated, but they would have to do as I had overspent on the shoes and outfit. Apart from these tights I had only brought with me a pair of black ones which would not work at all.

Suddenly my insides went cold: I had forgotten to buy a wedding present. My plan had been to buy a calendar for the month we were in which was November. A calendar made of fabric, a work of art really, but where would I find such a calendar and for only one month? Anyway there wasn't the time to go into town and look for one. Then I remembered the Chinese mugs, translucent white porcelain, decorated with delicate Oriental designs; red, black and gold, each had a lid with a small gold covered knob. One mug slightly larger than the other, his and hers. When you held them towards the light and looked inside them you could see the delicate relief of a woman's head. My father had brought them back from the Orient many years ago, perhaps sixty. I cannot remember a time when they were not standing on the shelf by the stove in the sitting room. Of course, I could wrap them up nicely and use them as a wedding present. They were precious; the gold on the knob and the calligraphy was real. Besides Adam and Samy appreciated anything that Granddad had brought back from his travels. So I started to get dressed; put on the skirt, then the tights. There were ladders in them; I couldn't wear those to my son's wedding. No problem, I would wear the other pair. Two young women, students of mine, pointed out that those had holes in them as well. It would have to be the black ones then, but they clashed with the delicate outfit and shoes! Nothing else for it, I had to go to the shops to buy new tights, but the shops were an hour's walk away and I didn't drive. If I walked there and back I would miss the ceremony. Somebody would have to drive me, but who? I ran around looking for someone to give me a lift, pink skirt, pink shoes, black tights. I caught a glimpse of myself in a mirror; I had forgotten to put on the lovely top and was still in the green t-shirt I had been wearing since the morning. But where was my exquisite top?

There ended the dream and I woke up in the soft semi-darkness of my bedroom in London. It was already after seven. I had not thought about the mugs for years. I can see them clearly now, standing proudly on the white shelf next to the wood-burning stove, so delicate it never occurred to any of us actually to use them for tea.

John and Åse were not happy to take over our parents' house as they already had a large and beautiful house on the opposite side of the lake. The area where they used to live was more populated and they got on well with their neighbours. In short, they had no wish to take over the old house where we had grown up and where Mum had lived on her own for close to twenty years. The neighbours told me they would watch her pottering about by herself, picking redcurrants in the garden, raking up dead leaves, keeping everything in order. The house was her life. It was Dad's vision that the house must always remain in the family, his legacy if you like. John and Åse knew that refusing to take it over would break Mum's heart and Dad would turn in his grave. I was out of the equation as I lived in England, so grudgingly John and Åse sold their large beautiful home and moved in.

Dad had designed the house to fill the long hours at sea during the war. Days in the midst of the ocean, in convoys, transporting oil for the Allies. Or, perhaps not so much when he was actually at sea with German warplanes and submarines relentlessly battering the convoys, but when his ship was in dock, or in quieter waters, which also happened. Something to hold on to, a way of keeping his sanity, who knows.

My father and his ship, Herbrand, went where they were ordered to go. Only once did he disobey orders. That was when the German Wehrmacht attacked Norway on April 9th 1940 and the Norwegian traitor and Nazi puppet, Vidkun Quisling, sent out his edict to the captain of every Norwegian ship in foreign waters to sail to German, Italian or neutral ports and join in the German war effort. My father, like the 1,000 other captains in the Norwegian commercial fleet, ignored the order and joined Nortraship and sailed under Allied command instead. Herbrand was in Port Arthur, Texas, at the time and set sail for Trinidad the following day. And so began five long years when Dad could not get back to his family in Norway and with no communication or news of how they were getting on. Five years spent going backwards and forwards across the Atlantic and the Indian Ocean, between New York and Britain and between India and the Persian Gulf. He sailed to other places as well, such as Sierra Leone; and most notoriously, and with the heaviest heart—to Murmansk as part of the dreaded arctic convoys, the most dangerous and hardest hit of all.

I don't know much about his life during those years. It happened before I was born and he never spoke about his experiences, except for personal anecdotes that he told us so many times that we stopped listening. I knew that he was one of the youngest but also one of the best captains in the Norwegian merchant fleet. I knew that he had sailed in convoys and that there were times when the Germans had sunk most of the ships and Dad's ship had been among the few to arrive at their destination, but I had little idea of what a convoy looked like. I imagined that it was a long line of ships and didn't know that a convoy could consist of up to 70 ships sailing in strict formation, several ships wide, with a fixed distance between each ship. Nor did I know that the convoys were protected by armed military ships and sometimes by military planes or that merchant ships were equipped with guns often manned by professional gunners. I had little idea about all this until I started researching it nearly 70 years later.

And why did I not know anything about his life during the war? Because Dad hardly spoke about it. Exactly why I'll never know. Trying to work it out would be ineptly applied psychological theories about the effects of long term stress and trauma. Pointless guesswork in other words.

By the time I was old enough to take in the wider world it was all ancient history to me, and my own life had taken over. Besides I was a dreamer, interested in books and music. Weapons and war held no fascination to me. Also, and this became a shameful blot on Norwegian history which refuses to go away: the sailors and their losses did not receive any recognition from the Norwegian authorities. I grew up on horror stories from the German occupation and the bravery of the resistance but heard little about the role of the sailors. If they had featured more in radio and

TV-programmes I would have ended up knowing more than I did. But they simply weren't mentioned. Still, Dad was proud of his contribution. He did tell us that Churchill had said that without the Norwegian sailors the Allied could not have won the war and that the Norwegian merchant fleet was worth more than a million soldiers. I have tried to find the exact quotes by Churchill, but all I have come up with is a quote by his transport minister, Philip Noel-Baker, to the same effect: "The First defeat for Hitler was The Battle of Britain. It was a turning point in history. If we had not had the Norwegian tankers on our side, we should not have had the aviation spirit to put the Hawker Hurricanes and Spitfires into the sky." I don't think Dad was aware of Philip Noel-Baker's statement, but knowing what Churchill had said infused him with a sense of pride that sustained him for the rest of his life.

So what do I know about his life during the war years? I know that he enjoyed listening to classical music because he brought home a collection of records that he had bought in various towns and cities that he had visited. I know about Tom, the ship's cat, who had appeared from somewhere and settled in my father's quarters and who was so clever that he used my father's toilet. I know that Dad filled the hours when nothing was happening with designing the house he would build if he survived the war. A dream house, a family home passed down to his son, Bjørn, and his children. John and I had not been thought of. A fine house as it turned out; perched on top of a hill, striking and white, with a ground floor veranda and a first floor balcony and as a slight maritime touch, a semi-circular lounge and a round bathroom window. Shrubs and roses at the front. Apple trees, cherry trees and red and black currant bushes at the back. Behind it, the dense Nordic forest of fir trees. I would so love to spend time there again but John and Åse can't stand people staying with them, not even me, so these days I stay with my good friend, Anne-Lise. She only lives next door, so I still get to wake up to the breath of the forest.

Most of Mum's and Dad's treasured belongings have been put in the attic. Some have been sold on e-bay and some have ended up in my nephews' houses.

In early January 2000, the last time my sons and I stayed in the house, I had the good sense to pack what I could into a large cardboard box and bring it to England—mainly candle holders and ornaments of crystal and glass such as the ship in the bottle. Other items; like the pseudo rococo chairs that mum embroidered ended up in Kai's house, which is fine. The nephews all wanted the house but none of them were economically ready to take it over and buy out the rest of us, so the burden, as John puts it, fell on him. He was referring to flaking paint and plaster work, rotting window frames and a hopelessly old-fashioned kitchen, among other things.

But the question remains: What became of the Chinese mugs that I had forgotten all about until this morning when I suddenly remembered them in a dream?

The white house on the hill

The Horse

There is one episode from my father's early life that he told us so many times that I can see it as clearly as if I had been there myself. The episode became part of his family's folklore and caused endless discussions between my father who said it happened when he was three, his sisters who thought he must have been older and those who were doubtful about whether it took place at all.

My father grew up in a small fishing village, or rather settlement named Hoddevik on the western extremity of Norway on a peninsula called Stadt. The lay-out of the place is unique. An ice-age glacier carved out a short valley in a perfect U-shape culminating in a sandy beach from where the North Atlantic stretches all the way to America. To the left of the beach there is an enormous sand dune also left by the westbound glacier. A narrow road links the village to the outside world, snaking its way down the mountainside in sharp hairpin bends. When it reaches the bottom it continues in a straight line in the middle of the U until it reaches the seafront where it ends. All the houses and out-buildings are spread out along the road like beads on a string. Each farm has a more or less identical strip of land across the valley. The village is surrounded by high treeless mountains on three sides and the open Atlantic on the fourth. My father's farm is situated in the middle and has been in his family from time immemorial. The oldest records date back to 1603 but the farm and the family go back further than that. The records were kept at the vicarage and one fine Sunday in 1603, whilst the vicar was in the pulpit, his wife went mad and set fire to the vicarage and all the records perished. The house where my father grew up is still there. It doesn't look particularly large from the outside, but being intended to house an extended family it has a surprising number of rooms.

* * *

So there he was my dad, Kristoffer Martin Elias Hoddevik, a little ginger-haired boy of three in grey home-spun clothes. If he was three, the year would have been 1905, when Norway got its independence from Sweden, but little Kristoffer knew nothing about that, nor did it matter to the people around him, their lives went on, fishing and working the land irrespective of who ran the country.

* * *

A sunny morning in mid-autumn. Last night little Kristoffer had heard his father say that it was time they got the mare down from the mountain pastures. The following morning Kristoffer woke up before his older brother who was sleeping in the same bed. Their mother was already in the cowshed milking and his father had gone off fishing. His father was a strict and serious man who never wasted his breath on idle chatter. I see him as a stern and somewhat distant father who sat down for his meals and then disappeared out again, to get in the hay, to fix something in the barn or to go fishing, often for days on end. By the time I knew him he was a very old man who hardly spoke at all, at least not to John and me; possibly because he was uncomfortable with our East-Norwegian accents, thinking that we wouldn't understand him, in fact I once heard him say so. Be that as it may. This morning little Kristoffer thought: I can go and get the mare, that will make Father happy, I'll go right now and when he gets back the mare will be here, and he will stroke my head and say: 'That's a good boy, you're a proper man now.' He'll be so pleased with me. He might even let me go fishing with him. So off he went. Nobody saw him leave and up the mountainside he climbed. He didn't follow the road but climbed in a more or less straight line. Had his mother and older brother discovered that he was missing and were running around looking for him? Very likely but he knew nothing about that. He kept plodding on higher and higher. Down below him the houses looked smaller. In many places water came trickling out of the ground. He was thirsty but it didn't occur to him that he could drink it. There were huge brown snails that he had never seen before and he had to stop and look at them. He saw blueberries that he couldn't help eating. Up and up he climbed until the mountain flattened and he reached the peat moors on top stretching out before him as far as he could see. And there was the old fallow mare, fat from the fresh grass she'd been eating. Kristoffer got up on her back and rode her all the way home. And so a family anecdote was born.

* * *

How he managed to sit on the horse's back, small as he was and without a saddle is a mystery. When asked he replied that the mare was old and sensible and walked carefully and that he held on to her mane.

'But how did you get up on her back when you were only three?' we'd ask him.

'I climbed up on a large boulder first and from there I climbed onto her back.'

'You must have been more than three.'

'No, I was three, and don't you come and tell me otherwise for you weren't even there.'

And so the argument would continue. I remember it well. However, thinking logically, if he was three he must have been closer to four, which is at least something. He was born on January 6th. They needed their horses on the farm during harvesting time, so the horses did not get up to the mountain pastures until mid-August, at the earliest. And the mare had been up there for a while so we're probably talking late September-early October which means he must have been three and about nine months, but even so . . .

* * *

Most likely he was between five and six, but somewhere along the line the idea that he was three got into his head and stuck there until he believed it himself. But who knows . . . The horse belonged to a small and sturdy breed called a Fjord Horse, so it was not like climbing on to a large shire horse, for example. Beautiful and good natured, all of them the same fallow colour.

By all accounts my father was an enterprising little lad. One of his sisters told me the following story: It was a windy day with rain and a fresh breeze from the south-west. The boys, my father and his younger brother, Oluf, were pottering about the yard as was their habit. Their mother, Petra, kept a vague eye on them. The next time she checked on them they were no longer in the yard. There were plenty of places they might have got to, but to be on the safe side she thought she'd better have a look around. They could be in the hay loft, they might be in the cowshed looking at the new calf or they might have gone to the pigsty to watch the pig wallowing in its muddy pen. But they were in none of these places and that was when Petra began to panic. Could they have fallen in the river? There is a small river or rather a brook running through the village. Not very big, but deep enough for a child to drown, especially in rainy weather like today. She ran to the river, called their names, followed the river a good way through the meadows. No sign of them. Only one more possibility, the worst. They must have gone to the seashore to watch the waves. She ran to the sea and there they were, standing on the edge of a cliff, white waves crashing in all around them, sopping wet, their cheeks red, their eyes shining with excitement. It was a miracle no wave had swept them away. Kristoffer got a good hiding then. It had to be his idea. Oluf was two years younger and not half as enterprising as his older brother.

Because of it openness this is one of the most treacherous and stormy stretches of water along the whole of the long Norwegian coast. (Photo, Magnhild Hoddevik)

Life in this western extremity of Norway was tough, but people were proud and self-sufficient. They owned their land, unlike country folk in eastern Norway who were often tenant farmers. Hoddevik looks beautiful on a warm summer's day, but such days can be few and far between. In winter gales and storms are the norm with enormous waves lashing against the shore. Over the centuries many a ship has been splintered against the sharp cliffs of this treacherous coastline. After a serious storm the villagers would collect driftwood, and other things that might come in handy.

The sea gave and it took. Scratching a living from the meagre land wasn't easy. In summer people would collect every blade of grass for winter fodder, whilst the animals, cows, sheep and goats were up in the mountain. Every morning and evening the women would somehow get up on the mountain to do the milking, either on foot or several of them sitting huddled together on a horse-drawn cart. By the time I started visiting Hoddevik they mostly went by tractor, several women on an open trailer behind the tractor. My mother said that these bedraggled women in their head scarves, sitting on the edge of a trailer dangling their feet, were the saddest sight. She had grown up not far from Oslo where life was easier and nature was kinder.

Even so the animal husbandry did not provide people with enough to live on and the rest of their livelihood had to be pulled out of the sea. It often happened that men went out fishing, were overcome by a storm and never seen again.

My paternal grandmother, Petra, grew up in a small settlement called Fure, a cluster of 4 - 5 houses on the other side of the mountain. From Hoddevik you could get there either by boat or by a tough climb across the mountain. They were quite wealthy at Fure because there was good salmon fishing. My grandmother's house is large and handsome and still in the family. I only visited it twice. There were fine silver goblets on the sideboards and mantelpieces, supposedly brought by Christine, a Danish aristocrat who somehow ended up in this isolated part of Norway in the late 18th century. They were two sisters but one of them died. The surviving sister married a local farmer/fisherman and made her home on this remote outpost. She had several children. One of her daughters married into my father's family which means that I am her direct descendant. Else, a cousin of mine and respected local historian, still living in Fure, tells me that as Christine's daughter married into my father's family in Hoddevik rather than in Fure, it means that the silver goblets I saw in my grandmother's house could not have originated from her. Pity, I liked to believe that Christine had brought them with her from Denmark. Whether she really was an aristocrat is an open question. However, the idea that we have aristocratic blood has stuck with the family ever since and given us a strong sense of pride and identity.

* * *

In this harsh climate the dead were never far away and many stories are told about them playing an active part in people's lives. There was for example the sexton who was clearing new land to expand the graveyard. The ground was full of large stones and boulders. The sexton had to lever the boulders out of the ground but they were too heavy for him to manage alone. So whilst using all his strength he said: 'Come on everyone!' meaning the dead. And up came the boulders, they were so large that no man could possibly have lifted them out on his own. My father saw them.

Another story my father used to tell also took place in the past, but still within living memory when he was a child: When the men from Hoddevik were out fishing and were surprised by bad weather, they would leave their boats at Fure, walk home across the mountain and walk back for their boat when the weather improved. That's also what happened this time. A team of six men had pulled their boat up on dry land and walked home across the mountain. One Sunday night a servant girl called Rasmina went to fetch water from the brook. That was when she saw the men from Hoddevik coming down the mountainside, but there were only five of them. They were carrying their leather clothes, the oil clothes of the day, and made their way down to their boat. She didn't see any more of them, nor did they come to the house and ask to stay the night, and the boat remained in place. On Monday morning the six men arrived and took to the sea to pull in their fishing nets. They caught a lot of fish. But then a storm blew up from the south-west. They hadn't got very far when the boat filled with water and every man was lost except one who somehow managed to sur-vive. The most interesting thing is that the girl saw the five men the day **before** they perished, like a warning of what was to come. I think this is both scary and comforting. Seeing an event before it takes place means that everything is planned, and what is meant to happen will. Although there are times when our lives hang in the balance and the pendulum can swing either way, but more about that later.

The belief in help from above and beyond the grave is deeply ingrained in the population of this treacherous coastline, and a certain psychic ability runs in our family. My father always "knew" when there were German

U-boats in the nearby waters, a sixth sense that helped him and his crew to survive the war.

* * *

Throughout my childhood and youth we always visited Hoddevik in summer when Dad was on leave, and I loved it. I loved the sand dune where I used to roam around picking wildflowers. I loved the sandy beach where I could stand for ages watching the surf breaking against the shore or I would collect beautiful seashells, dreaming of England and the Faroe Islands and America beyond the horizon. I remember feeling sad that such a perfect beach should be lying unused. The people of Hoddevik had never had time for frivolities like swimming and sunbathing. Many of them couldn't even swim. One of God's mistakes, I thought, to place a beautiful sandy beach where nobody would enjoy it. Looking at the clean green water I very much wanted to go swimming but nobody wanted to come with me. I did swim there on my own once or twice. The water was fresh and crystal clear, but ice cold. The second and last time I ventured into the water the breaking waves were so strong that they knocked me over and when I got up another wave knocked me right down, winding me and filling my mouth and nose with salty water. I was glad to reach dry land and never ventured into that icy sea ever again. Often I would hang about with my cousin, Marit. She was eight years older than me, but didn't seem to mind having me around. She would show me rare plants and sea anemones, or we would sit together painting and drawing. I was known to be quite good, but Marit was much better and it wasn't only due to the age gap. Marit's drawings had something extra. I watched in amazement as she quickly sketched perfect images of flowers and people around her—and the way she copied famous paintings so well that you could hardly see the difference . . . I looked at it all and realized that I would never be that good. She knew English and could tell me what the English pop songs we heard on the radio were about, and I was very impressed. She only stayed on the farm during summer. In winter she was away at school or college. In this remote outpost of western Norway with its scattered population there were no secondary schools around the corner or a short bus-ride away like where I lived. Anyone who wanted more than elementary education had to go away and live in digs closer to their school.

The sandy beach of Hoddevik. (Photo, Magnhild Hoddevik)

Things change. These days Hoddevik has become known as a surfer's paradise. I found this description on the Internet: *Sandy beach between towering mountains on the westernmost part of mainland Norway. Hoddevik is very popular for surfers from all over the world. In Nordfjord Hoddevik is the best spot in west-swells. Hoddvik is also very good under extremely windy conditions due to the tall mountains surrounding the spot and protecting it from heavy winds.*

I also came across an article about it in an in-flight magazine published by Norwegian Air, where the fishing village is described as the most beautiful place in Norway. And of course the surfers have wetsuits protecting them from the icy water.

Kristoffer Martin Elias Hoddevik, who was he?

Kristoffer Martin Elias Hoddevik, the second oldest son on a small farm in Western Norway. After him came one more brother, a girl named Augusta plus four more girls. Augusta died at seven months; she suffocated under her blanket. My grandmother never got over it and kept an ever watchful eye on her subsequent children and later on her grandchildren and great grandchildren. Law and tradition dictated that the oldest son should inherit the farm, the younger sons had to go out into the world and carve out their own future, which many of them did admirably well. After completing elementary school in the village the daughters usually remained on the farm until they married a local farmer/fisherman, or they went into service in Bergen or Ålesund. In this my grandparents were different. They educated their daughters, sending three of them off for further education, which in those days was unusual. Why they all chose nursing as a career I don't know. Economy must have played a part; there certainly wasn't much money in the family and a student nurse would get free board and lodgings plus a tiny allowance, or perhaps it sprang from a genuine desire to do good. Besides there were fewer occupations open to girls in those days. The fourth sister, Maria, married a local farmer and had three children. Her older son, Halvdan, took over the farm. He was a man of great intellectual capacity who spoke fluent English, but renounced what could have been a glittering career to keep up the ancestral farm, the outermost farm in Hoddevik and next to the sandy beach. In later life he was instrumental in attracting surfers to the village and opened a kiosk on the beach. Maria's daughter, Marit, that I so admired as a child, did indeed become an artist turning everything she touched into works of art, and as she got older became increasingly eccentric. People often talked about her projects and her eccentricities as when she ordered a special breed of sheep from Shetland because she wanted to make felt from their wool and turn it into some kind of wall-hangings. The sheep arrived—beautiful animals with long silky fleece. But, it had not occurred to Marit to make an enclosure for them and the sheep had no idea about the difference between indoors and outdoors so they would wander into the house leaving presents on the floor and eating Marit's pot plants.

I learned about this from my mother who had it from Auntie Astrid. Marit did complete some wall-hangings; a lengthy and messy process involving a lot of water, but as far as I know the project was short-lived.

Mum also told me about another episode which was quite amusing and which she could only have heard from Marit's own mouth: Apart from being an artist Marit also worked full-time as a teacher. She was married to a local fisherman and had four children, so one may wonder how she managed to do any artwork at all. When she was in Oslo, which was not very often, she would go to as many art galleries and exhibitions as possible. Sometimes she would take Auntie Astrid with her for company. Once they visited an exhibition by Norway's most renowned painter, Norway's answer to David Hockney if you like. They had not expected to find the great master in person, but there he was. Marit couldn't believe her luck. Coming from a small place in the West Country and being known only locally, she had to pluck up all her courage to go over and talk to him, which was when it became apparent that the fêted artist was somewhat the worse for wear, although not scandalously so, and Marit was too delighted to mind. But Auntie Astrid thought differently. She kept pulling at Marit's arm whispering loud and clear: 'Marit, don't talk to him. Marit, come away from him. Come on, Marit, can't you see that he's drunk!' Marit was furious but what could she do? Her big moment had been well and truly ruined.

Her younger brother, Arne, became a sea captain like my father and later on he worked on an oil rig in the North Sea. He married an American woman and took up residence in the South-Country.

In short; a clan of intelligent and gifted people who knew the value of hard work. They shed their country bumpkin image, modified their dialect and became successful citizens of the wider world. My grandfather's younger brother became the director of Oslo's main secretarial college. For some reason he lost touch with the family. At least I had never heard of him until he died and a beautiful bureau of dark wood with a fold-out flap and drawers in different sizes suddenly came to my father. Objects were important and had to find a home within the family once their owner had passed away.

But my father, Kristoffer Martin Elias Hoddevik, who was he really? Who is any of us, come to that. We are what people see, our background, our actions, our occupation, the way we look, but that's not the full story.

I have many memories of my father, but none of them tells me who exactly the larger-than-life Captain who could stand on the bridge for three days and nights in a row really was. When I say larger than life I mean personality-wise, not physically. He was tall and sturdy, but not unusually so. His stature was more in his demeanour, the air of authority that clung to him like a well-fitting cloak, not somebody you'd want to argue with. They called him the Iron Man for his ability to remain on duty on the bridge for as long as it took, standing still, his eyes scouring the sea for a periscope or a torpedo trail. He did the Murmansk Run at least twice, possibly more often—the most dangerous route of all, and with a ship full of oil . . . One direct hit and the Herbrand would have exploded in flames and only the very lucky ones would have survived. He saw sinking ships belching flames and smoke. At night he could see the red distress lights on the life jackets of sailors from stricken ships who had ended up in the water. The order was clear: Don't stop to pick up survivors, a ship that stops, is a target and might cause a collision. The worst thing was ploughing your way through a sea of desperate men doomed to die without being able to help them and knowing that the next time it might be you. Sometimes the Herbrand would act as escort oiler, which meant fuelling an escorting warship. This was extremely dangerous as it required both ships to be stationary throughout the process, making them both an easier target.

30

What had it all done to him? By the time I was born he would have had time to adjust back to normality, if that was at all possible. Perhaps he'd managed to put it all well and truly behind him; as he never spoke about it, I shall never know ... At any rate it was business as usual. Out sailing the world for nineteen months at a time, then back home for three months. This was to become a pattern that lasted throughout my childhood and most of my teenage years until he was invalided home when I was sixteen. More about that later. My mother would nag him to do odd jobs around the house, which he resisted and only started the day before he was due to leave, and consequently didn't manage to finish and the job would remain half-done till the next time he came home close to two years later. He was older than most fathers, and didn't engage in any sort of play with John and me. And, as it turned out; had little idea about being young in the late 1960s-early70s, complaining about John's pop-music and my clothes, finding my skirts too short and my tops too tight and revealing. I would insist that only "sad" girls wore their skirts below their knees, to which he retorted: 'Then be sad, then!' The battle against his teenage children was one where he had to admit defeat. I'm sure he loved us in his way, but his real love was the sea.

February 2013

It is uncanny how most things you see and do—things that seem trivial at the time—will one day come in handy. An overheard snippet of a conversation on the Tube can provide a piece of information that might turn out to be useful. A letter or a photo can survive for years in the bottom of a drawer; get stuffed into a box during a house move only to end up in the bottom of a different drawer until finally it crops up just when you need it.

Here I am in my house in South London trying to piece together a part of my father's life that took place before I was born and of which I have only scant information. When he told his anecdotes and stories—things that had happened to him or his men, it was often without specifying where or when they had taken place and it seldom occurred to us to ask. Nor was it important; it had happened somewhere out there, in the big wide world and little did it matter whether it was in Buenos Aires or Caracas.

I'm looking at a photo that has been considered important enough to be cartered around from drawer to drawer for seventy years. How did it get into my possession? I came across it in January 2000 whilst rifling through the bureau that my father had inherited from his uncle. I saw nothing wrong in this. Dad was long gone and Mum was in a nursing home. Soon John and Åse would be taking over the house and change everything to their taste, so why shouldn't I collect a few mementos for myself and my sons. It was the day after our legendary party and Adam and Samy had gone to dinner at Kai's whilst I stayed home to pack what I could into a cardboard box to take to England with me. A good job too as it turned out. Instead of languishing in the attic being covered in dust and possibly broken, or sold on eBay, these objects have pride of place in my home. The photo, however, got put in a drawer and ignored for 13 years when it suddenly surfaced, and this is how it happened:

I was searching through a drawer looking for the receipt of a watch that might still be under guarantee, and which I didn't find. What did turn up was a picture that I vaguely remembered having seen a long time ago—a faded black and white photo most likely taken by some harbour photographer: It had postcard lines on the back and Dad's handwriting and read: *To Bjørn from papa. This was taken in Buenos Aires, at the quayside of the famous Boca. From the left: me, the First Engineer, the First Officer and the Second Engineer.* That's all it said, no date to indicate when it was taken. The four men are all hatted and suited, white shirt and tie, polished dark shoes. Dad, slightly taller than the other three, is carrying an overcoat over his left arm. The Second Engineer has a coat slung over his shoulder. Four gentlemen out to paint the town. My father looks younger than I remember him and he was 46 when I was born. Being with his First Officer tells me that he was the Captain of the ship. He got his first command around 1940 so most likely the photo was taken during the War at the start of a night out—precious respite from the ever present threat of German bomber-planes, submarines and warships out on the open sea. But this is guesswork, I can't know for sure. From anecdotes that he told us I have gathered he was in Buenos Aires a few times. He spoke of going to a meat restaurant called La Cabaña. Recently I searched for it on the Internet on the off chance that it's still there, and it is: *Restaurante de Carnes*, photos, location and all!

Examining the photo it suddenly strikes me: I have been there! I have walked along exactly that quayside, only at the time I had no idea that Dad had walked there some seventy years before me!

How did I come to be in Boca? Maher and I were on a package-tour of Chile, Argentina and Brazil. We landed in Buenos Aires around 10am and were met by our local guide, a burly man in his 30s whose name I've forgotten. Directly outside the airport building was the sea, no islands, no piers, just an infinite expanse of yellowish-brown water, the colour of milky tea, lapping against the side of the road only meters away from the building; choppy, some waves were white crested. A totally unexpected sight. I said to Andrew, our tour leader, 'I didn't realise that Buenos Aires is directly on the seafront.'

'No, it isn't the seafront; it's a river, the River Plate.'

Oh, the famous Rio de la Plata! But why call it the River Plate? I wish he would have pronounced the name properly instead of this watered-down anglicised version.

Anyway . . . Rio de la Plata, the Silver River . . . a river I had heard of and read about but never thought I would get to see. The widest river in the world, you can't see across it. A natural border between Argentina and Uruguay. Not very deep, only about three meters. The silt has to be dug out to make passages for large ships. This has to be done continuously. Only now do I realise that Dad must have passed where I was standing many times. What a pity I didn't think of this when I was there.

The coach took us to la Recoleta Cemetary to see the final resting place of Eva Peron, a necropolis where rich families have mausoleums, a desert of stone and concrete. Eva is incarcerated in a deep vault with other members of her family. People still remember her and attach fresh flowers to the outside wall.

Our local guide seemed distracted, his heart not in it. Andrew explained that later in the day there would be a match between the two main Argentinian football teams, Boca and River Plate, and that our guide was keen to get home to watch it.

After the cemetery we went to la Boca, a poor but pleasant-looking district with colourful houses, many of them with brightly painted corrugated iron. The streets are tree-lined and many houses are decorated with street art, mainly stylized paintings of people. Originally and still mostly an Italian neighbourhood. We were let off the bus and told that we had two hours to ourselves. Being ignorant about football la Boca meant nothing to me. I must have seen it at the back of Dad's card but it had failed to register. Even Maher, who enjoys football, couldn't understand what we were doing here when there were plenty of more interesting places to see. It was lunch time. We found a café with a large outside seating area, a workman's caff really, raucous and crowded, but it was the only eating place in sight. Quite a few other members of our group ate there as well. We ordered sandwiches which, when they finally arrived, turned out to be not bad at all; chunky slices of fresh white bread with lots of yellow cheese and olives.

Having finished our meal with time to spare, we pottered around for a while before making our way along the quayside to the place where the coach would be waiting. The area was full of arty people and souvenir stalls, reminiscent of London's Camden. Nobody in our group seemed aware that to serious football fans this was Mecca and neither Andrew nor the local guide had thought to explain it. Most likely taking it for granted that we all knew and were delighted to set foot there. Only now do I realise that Dad's photo was taken in the very spot where I so reluctantly found myself some 70 years later. If only I'd known at the time . . .

We drove past la Boca Football Stadium. It's painted blue and yellow like the Swedish flag, owing to some connection to Sweden that I didn't quite get. There was a steady stream of people on their way to watch the match which would start in a couple of hours.

Typical scene from La Boca

We did stop at the Plaza de Mayo in front of the Pink Palace where Eva Peron made her famous address to the people. This is where the mothers and grandmothers of "Los Desaparecidos" (the Disappeared) hold a vigil every Thursday. The idea is to demonstrate that they have not given up hope of finding out what happened to their loved ones who were snatched off the streets during the reign of the Junta, 1976—1983, or to be reunited with them. The women in their white head scarves have become an enduring symbol of hope and desire for justice. The coach stopped by the Plaza but unbelievably we were only given ten minutes. Maher and I wanted photos of the Pink Palace and of the ring of white scarves painted on the cobble stones. It wasn't a Thursday so we didn't see any mothers and grandmothers. Time flew. When we looked at our watches we saw that our ten minutes were up and hurried back to the coach where everybody was already seated and we got angry looks from Andrew and the guide.

At our hotel we were given vouchers towards a meal at a nearby meat restaurant, not *La Cabaña* but similar, judging by the photos I saw on the Internet. It was a type of restaurant seldom seen in Europe any more, like stepping back in time—dark wood panelling, stuffed animal heads on the walls, waiters in black trousers and white jackets. We shared a table with two people from our group, an older woman with her toy-boy we assumed, who turned out to be mother and son. Maher and the mother and son had the most enormous steaks I have ever seen. I eat very little meat, but there was no proper vegetarian option, only a mozzarella salad, which was nice enough.

My father would eat meat as long as it was clean meat, either steak or roast, or my mother's beef in a spicy sauce, one of her specialities, which he trusted. Everybody loved Mum's beef in sauce, and that is all it was, beef and sauce seasoned with salt, black pepper, tomatoes and sometimes brown goat's cheese. It might have been in Buenos Aires, but not in *La Cabaña,* that Dad had an experience that put him off meat casseroles for life. It was definitely somewhere in Latin America. He was at a restaurant and a pot of spicy meat stew was put in front of him. It was delicious, one of the best dishes he'd ever tasted, tender pieces of meat with exotic vegetables in a pungent sauce. He'd had two platefuls and was helping himself to a third, when up came a piece of fur, a rat that had fallen into the cooking pot. It turned his stomach so violently that he rushed out and was sick. For the rest of his life he refused to eat anything where he couldn't see exactly what he was eating. Except for Mum's beef in sauce.

On our second day in Buenos Aires we went to El Tigre, an optional excursion but everybody in our group seemed to be on the coach, like us they must have realised that it was the best way to get something out of the day. It is difficult to navigate your way around Buenos Aires if you are there for the first time. Everything is larger than life; the widest river in the world and I think the widest avenue with its seven lanes in each direction. The parks are enormous. There are clusters of modern sky scrapers, an intimidating world of concrete and glass, not somewhere you would go for a stroll. The tree-lined avenues stretch on for ever, and these I did like the look of. They have a European, old worldly feel about them. I would have liked to have gone to one such avenue, found a pavement café, had a snack and simply sat. We saw these avenues from the coach but to find them under our own steam would be difficult as we didn't know what they were called.

So, we joined the excursion to El Tigre, a small town north of Buenos Aires situated on an island on the delta of the Paraná River. From there we went on a boat trip around the Delta, a wetland created by a multitude of little islands made up of silt from the Paraná. When the first Spaniards reached the area they saw the jaguars who lived there at the time and not knowing any better thought they were tigers, hence the name, El Tigre.

The local guide was on the coach but like yesterday there wasn't much he wanted to tell us, except that Buenos Aires is the second largest urban area in South America after São Paulo, that so and so many square metres are taken up by parks and so on. What did I see that day? Driving along-side one of the many parks I saw a man with thirteen dogs on a lead. Soon after I saw another man sitting on the grass with a similar band of dogs tied to a tree. Andrew explained that the men were professional dog walkers, taking dogs whose owners were working for walks. I hate to think what would happen if they all started fighting, but they seemed peaceful enough, coasting along like well-disciplined school children. What else did I see? An old man in a purple anorak walking two dachshunds, two rich ladies coming out of a designer shop, their cloths super-expensive and art-fully put together—Mulberry and Louis Vuitton handbags—not one hair out of place . . .

Then there was the water-world. The boat making its way between seemingly endless little islands. The same tea-coloured water as in Rio de la Plata. Lush vegetation. Houses painted bright blue, green or yellow. Some on stilts, the water lapping at their feet, some further inland surrounded by palm-trees and opulent greenery. Grand villas with ornate details, con-servatories and large windows, reminiscent of the painted wooden houses from the early 20th century that we find in northern Europe. However, these must be made of more durable stuff. Wood wouldn't last five minutes in this wetland. The people who live out here are well healed—a para-dise to come home to after a day in a tower block office. Little wooden piers for private use, some with plastic bags of household rubbish tied to a pole. A dustcart-boat would pick them up later. We passed two grocery boats loaded with soft drinks and essentials. The boats pull up by the piers and people come down and do their shopping. For a while an expensive speedboat with a beautiful 30-something woman at the helm came trundling behind us. Next to her sat an 11 - 12 year old boy. The woman had a scarf tied over her head. After a while she speeded up and overtook us. As she zoomed past I noticed that she had long brown hair right down to her waist. Later, back on solid ground I saw a woman of advanced years. She had long swept-back blond hair, lots of eye make-up and raspberry coloured lipstick. Very petite. Weird black trousers and a beige knitted top. She looked beautiful even if she must have been long past 70.

Seeing my face and figure reflected in shop windows in these unfamiliar surroundings I realize that I look older and heavier that I imagined. I honestly believed that I'd managed to hang on to a remnant of my good looks. I now realize this is not so. This last winter has been a terrible slog; relentless teaching, marking and boring meetings. It has taken away the last vestiges of my youth. As Rose Tremain put it: *Old age arrives in short flurries. Between the flurries there is a kind of respite.* Seems I have been through one such flurry. But with sensible eating, make-up and the right clothes I should be abler to stave off the worst ravages of age for a few more years. Seeing a beautiful woman much older than me has given me hope.

* * *

What more did I see? From the coach, just before midnight, returning from a tango show, I saw people rifling through black rubbish bags that had been left outside restaurants, looking for something to eat.

* * *

We are back at the airport, leaving Buenos Aires. Andrew talking into his microphone, loud sharp voice. I'm not really listening. Our plane has been delayed or cancelled, not sure which, same difference, same result; we're stuck here for an extra two hours. I say to Maher: 'Look at the river! It's so wide you can't see across it, the other side is Uruguay.' No reaction, he's talking to a man in our group who is here with his wife, both late middle age, both Indian and both doctors. Perhaps I should go to Uruguay one day. Around me people talking. I don't get it, what is there to talk about all the time? Maher talks more than anyone, talks and talks about politics, about football, about his theory why so many people are gay these days. Everybody's talking. I cannot be bothered. Talking ruins the most beautiful moments, cluttering up the silence with pointless noise. Never could understand this pleasure in talking for the mere sake of it, to verbalise every little thought that flutters through your mind, to talk about anything as long as it kills the threat of silence,—inane conversation about nothing. I'm happy as I am—standing by the large window watching the Silver River, listening to a song that's going round in my head. *La Foule.* I love the syncopated piano chords at the beginning. Edith Piaf brought it back from Latin America where she had been on tour. The song was promptly translated into French and Piaf made it a hit. A lady sang it on the tango show that we went to the other night. I was hoping for my favourite tango *La Comparasita* but it didn't come. My father must have bought it in South America during or before the War. It was in his record collection that he brought home with him, a heavy 75 record. I played it on his old wind-up gramophone. It was a bit scratched, its voyage from a distant world engraved in its grooves. Soon after we got a more modern record player and I played it on that one as well. The lazy and drawn-out summers of the 1950s. A safe world. You knew where you stood. Dreams and worries about the future had not yet entered my life. Me sitting on the floor by the gramophone, playing records. Door open onto the garden, onto the forest, onto the lake and the mountains on the horizon. Blue sky. No sound except for the music that I'm playing. Nobody disturbing me. My family leaving me to my own devices. Me playing *La Comparasita.*

It must have been out at sea, far out with no land in sight that my father had an experience that remained with him for life. Whether it was off Argentina or some other South American country doesn't matter. Like I've said before, Dad would tell his stories without specifying where and when. The main thing is that it happened and that my father was convinced they had received help from above. In his words: *We were off the coast of South America and it was a fine day with blue sky and brilliant sunshine and we were alone on the sea. The First Officer spotted a ship on the horizon. At first we didn't know what sort of ship it was, but it came nearer. We looked through the telescope and before long we could see that it was a small German warship. They were everywhere in those days patrolling the sea; their task was to sink lone Allied ships whenever they had the chance. And soon they would have the chance to sink us. We speeded up, but it was no good. The German was gaining on us fast. We were a sitting duck. Soon it would be within firing range, nothing we could do. Our days were numbered. But then, suddenly and out of nowhere came the heaviest rain and thunderstorm I have ever seen in my life. Visibility was down to zero, we couldn't see a thing. That was when I gave my order: 'Sharp starboard and full steam ahead.' Not long after the storm lifted as suddenly as it had come, and the day was as clean and clear as before. We scoured the horizon but the German was nowhere to be seen. We'd got away and we never saw him again.*

Some people are sceptics and when I tell them this story they argue that this is an area prone to sudden storms and that this was just one such storm. That may be, but Dad believed till his dying day that they had got help from above and that's what I believe too. I discussed this with Mum, who was not a religious woman, and she believed it: After Dad had passed away she said: 'There is power in prayers and your grandmother must have sent a lot of prayers to heaven to keep her boy safe.'

Sitting in my South London home with the February sun through my window, I realize that the people I noticed in Buenos Aires are still there, going about their business—the dog walkers walking their bands of dogs, the elderly man with his two dachshunds, the lady in the expensive speedboat, the beautiful 70-something woman . . . The two rich ladies are spending their mornings shopping, the poor people are scavenging for food. Real people, real lives of which I know nothing at all.

A Slow Boat
to China

What had motivated Kristoffer to make the journey from a small fishing community in western Norway to a fashionable meat restaurant in Buenos Aires? I put it down to intelligence, a resolute spirit and a background that gave him a good sense of self and instilled in him the value of hard and sustained work. Because of this he had little time for people who did not take their fate into their own hands but instead sat around waiting for their local council or their country to do it for them. Referring to the 1920s when times were hard and unemployment rife he used to say: 'When other men stood around on street corners and became communists, I took myself off to Canada, worked as a lumberjack and saved up money for my education.' I can picture him now, the boy from the sea in the frozen Canadian wilderness; working till his back nearly broke, quite literally. He did lasting damage to his back when lifting a log that was much too heavy.

One problem with having children later in life is that by the time the children grow up much of a parent's youth is lost in the mist of time. Besides, from children's perspectives anything that happened before they were born is ancient history especially when it took place 20, 30, 40 years ago. Thus, my knowledge of Dad's early adult life is limited. I know that he sailed on the whaling ships in the South Atlantic. Norway had a large whaling fleet back then and the idea that whales are magnificent creatures that should be protected had not yet occurred to anyone. Unlike many Norwegian men my father never took part in blood sports so I believe that he can't possibly have liked this work. It was a job that paid good money at a time when there wasn't much else going. All he ever told us about his

41

time in the southern seas is that he enjoyed watching the penguins on South Georgia—like posh men in dress shirt and tails discussing business.

Dad often spoke of his time on the banana boat, but without mentioning the boat's name. I assumed that it must have been before the war and before he became a captain, but recently John came across an old newspaper-cutting from a Brazilian paper that raised the banana boat from myth to reality. She was called M/S *Atlantic Express*, and was constructed in Landskrona, Sweden, in 1942 for the transportation of fruit between South America and Norway. She was laid-up during World War 2 and not put to sea till August 1st 1945. She was sold to a French firm in 1949 and renamed *Fort Duquesne*. Under yet another flag and another name she continued to sail the seas till March 20th 1970 when she arrived in Shanghai for demolition. The cutting has no date, but thanks to the Internet I can pinpoint my father's time on her to somewhere between 1945 and 1949. She could make the journey from Santos in Brazil to Norway in 14 days and 14 hours, and had comfortable cabins for passengers.

The article mentions *O Capitão Kristoffer Hoddevik*. It also tells of a lunch on board for men in the fruit-export business. There are two photographs, grainy and faded. A group photo with my father, his features barely discernible, in full uniform, sitting behind a rescue ring with *Atlantic Express, Oslo* written on it, and one from the lunch with my father at the head of the table. He loved the banana boat, as he called it, even though it was equipped for other types of fruit as well. It was painted white and kept shiny clean. Dad told us that bananas had to be treated with great care, transporting them was a science. They had to be kept hanging in a warm and dark storeroom. The temperature had to be constant. If it sank below a certain point the bananas would catch a chill and be ruined, so never put bananas in the fridge. Thanks to an old newspaper cutting and the Internet an obscure period in my father's life has been authenticated and given a time-frame.

He also mentioned some of the passengers. This was before the era of mass travel so people who travelled long distance usually did so for a reason. Individuals seeking a passage on cargo boats were not rich; otherwise they would have been on a large ocean-going liner. God knows via which byways of fate they had ended up 'slumming it' on a fruit boat from one side of the world to the other. Many of these passengers were fascinating individuals providing welcome distraction for the officers on long and monotonous crossings. Some of course, were less than fascinating—like an English couple my father sometimes spoke of. The husband had held a minor position at a British embassy somewhere and now they were returning to England, on a banana boat or it might have been a tanker. But they were posh. So posh that they turned their noses up at the food and barely deigned to speak to the officers, apart from my father, the captain. But Dad was nobody's fool and knew how to show them up, and they were too stupid to twig. Passengers took their meals with the officers. One day, at dinner, the posh couple had just said no thank you to a fish dish that they didn't like the look of. My father said to the officer sitting next to him: 'Amazing what a few spoons of good caviar does to the flavour, don't you think?' The wife heard it and her face lit up: 'Oh, caviar, let me try!'

Then there was the French countess. She must have made quite an impression for my father to still be talking about her many years later. During the day she wore khakis, one trouser-leg rolled up to below the knee and the other one hanging down, always. Her khaki shirt had two breast pockets; cigarettes in one, matches in the other. This at a time when upper class women wore pleated skirts, twinsets and pearls. But come dinnertime and she was every bit the countess—elegant dresses, jewellery, the lot. I've seen a photo of her, I think. My father used to keep a lot of black and white snapshots in a chocolate box. I looked through them once or twice and my eyes fell on a black and white photo of a woman—indeterminate age, large eyes, high forehead, chiselled nose, tied-back blondish hair, long ear-rings . . . . A striking face without being exactly beautiful, so different from the women I knew, exuding character and personality, although I couldn't have put such words on it back then. She was sitting at a table, cigarette between her fingers, next to a man. At the back of the photo Dad had written: *The Countess and Brian Fugelly.* It all seemed so exotic, so different from the ordinary folk around me—the women on the bus returning with their shopping—beige mac, short permed hair, plain and dreary, talking about the price of milk and potatoes. The woman in the photo ignited in me a burning desire to enter a world where I too would meet countesses and people with weird and wonderful names. One big difference though. My father wasn't in it for the sake of seeing exotic locations and meeting interesting people. He was in it because he loved the job, everything else was coincidental.

China

It took years but eventually I did get to travel and meet amazing individuals. I've been to China three times. The first was a spectacular tour following the Silk Route starting in Beijing and travelling by plane, coach, train and donkey all the way through the Gobi desert to the western extremity of China, and via the dangerous Karakoram highway to the Pakistani border. The magic of it all . . . In the desert we visited what had once been thriving cities but which now lay deserted, the houses and temples reverting to the sand that they sprung from. Streets where nobody had lived for hundreds of years. I'll never forget journeying through the desert and catching my first glimpse of snow-clad peaks suspended in the sky above the misty clouds—the Karakoram Mountains, pure magic.

My second visit was only short. Without Maher I had taken the Trans-Siberian Railway from Moscow to Beijing. In order to have a first class compartment to myself I had paid double and so could only afford one night in Beijing. Still, I was there, right before the start of the 2008 Olympics and in the space of one afternoon and evening I managed to cram in a lot, starting with a trip to the beautiful Temple of Heaven. I had been there on our first visit, but it is the sort of place you can visit again and again. It is surrounded by an enormous park, peaceful and dreamlike, full of trees and flowers. Next I had a meal in a restaurant where I and two men from Colombia, according to their T-shirts, were the only non-natives. The night was rounded off with a visit to the opera, watching a cross between an acrobatic and singing show.

To think that I once rode a camel in the Gobi Desert.
(Photo Wikimedia Commons)

In 2009 I was back with Maher. This time on a different organized tour also starting in Beijing and including a cruise on the Yangtze River before continuing to Tibet.

My father had been to China a few times. As with many of the places he visited he never told us exactly where or when. He did say that he had sailed up a Chinese river before the revolution, most likely the Yangtze from Shanghai. He said that it had been extremely fascinating and that he had never seen people living as miserably as the Chinese. He hated Communism as much as he hated Nazism; even so he said that anything that could give these people a better life had to be a good thing. No human being deserved to live like the Chinese he had observed from his ship. He must have been there later too because he brought home some exquisite Chinese items such as beautiful white silk pyjamas for me with large embroidered flowers. I remember a painted fan that I hung on the wall in my bedroom, one of the objects that have since been lost. There is the black tray with inlaid Chinese motifs in mother-of-pearl now residing on my mantelpiece. And of course—the two Chinese mugs that I haven't seen for years.

So here I am making my way through China with Maher, travelling with a group made up of British and Australian people in more or less equal numbers. Our tour leader is an effervescent thirty year old Chinese woman called Lisa who speaks excellent English. At each stop we are met by a local Chinese guide.

September 8th. Xian

Woke up during the night feeling not particularly good. Looked at the clock on my mobile. 3.05. Right now choir practice would be starting back in England. At least one person missing from the sopranos. Dense impenetrable darkness, dense headache. Too much brandy last night to knock myself out in order to get a night's sleep. The window is ajar but it feels like there is no oxygen in the room. We are on the 11th floor of a very modern hotel. It's so dark you can't see your hand when holding it up in front of you. That's because up here there are no street lights to dilute the darkness. This is how millions and millions of Chinese people live, crammed into tiny flats; 8, 9, 10 perhaps 20 floors, no balcony, no greenery, heavy and polluted atmosphere. The old Chinese way was to live close to the ground to absorb energies from the Earth, everybody used to know each other. In the modern high-rises they don't even know their next door neighbours.

Eventually I went back to sleep only to be woken up by the lights in the room suddenly coming on. It wasn't Maher's doing as he was fast asleep in the next bed. Soon after they switched off by themselves only to come back on five minutes later. For how long was this going to continue? By the light of my mobile I went to the door and took out the key card that controls the lights from its slot. Back to bed and back to sleep, strangely enough. Woke up at 5.21. Fine, I'd set my phone to ring at 5.45 so I might as well get up and have a shower. I put the key back in its slot. Immediately all the lights sprang into action. Looked for the switches, remembered there were none. All the lights were controlled from a touch panel between the beds. How they expect a person to find this panel and touch the right spot in total darkness is beyond me. Succeeded in switching off Maher's bedside lights. He was still asleep. He needed it, poor man. He dropped off several times last night during the Tang Dynasty Dance show, good as

47

it was. I nearly nodded off too. Evocative music, beautiful costumes and dancing—still I struggled to stay awake. The programme on this tour is simply too packed—from early morning till late at night.

After my shower, darkness finally receded to reveal thick fog, or perhaps smog. Small wonder I'd felt an acute lack of oxygen during the night.

Today the programme was to be woken up at 6.30. Breakfast at 7. Departure at 8. Too rushed for me. First stop; the Historic Museum, then a craft place where they make replica terracotta soldiers. I think it must be the same place we visited two years ago. After that lunch followed by the real Terracotta Army, followed by a visit to the Muslim quarter back in Xian followed by dinner at the hotel. Early rise tomorrow to pack and check out ready for our flight to Wuhan and a 5—6 hours' bus ride to join the boat for our Yangtze cruise.

We've done it! We've bunked off! Discovering the packed programme and getting increasingly exhausted from sleep deprivation and constantly being on the go, we decided to give the museum and the Terracotta Army a miss. We saw the Terracotta Army two years ago, and it's the sort of thing where once is enough. Once you've seen it, you've seen it. On top of the strenuous programme comes the strain of chattering Australians and Lisa doing her best to keep us entertained, giving us constant information much of which we forget due to tiredness and overload.

Our room is spacious: Two desks and chairs for writing. Near the window—a coffee table, a two-seater sofa and two matching deep arm-chairs. Some traffic noise rising from the street, mainly cars beeping.

Before going back to sleep Maher went down to reception to tell Lisa that we would not be coming on the excursion. He is not always sensitive to people's reactions so how Lisa had taken this breach in Chinese discipline, I'll never know. Those members of the group who had overheard reacted with a mixture of shock and envy. One of the Australian women, Wendy, an elegant lady of my age told him she wished she'd had the courage to do likewise because she was tired out. She's here with her husband. Can't remember his name, tall man with short grey hair, an inconspicuous sort of man. Wendy told me she doesn't like to walk around with him all the time. I said Maher and I are like that and sometimes even have separate holidays; better than to compromise. She replied that nothing is worse than a boring husband.

One aspect of China that I could never come to grips with is the lack of benches to sit and have a rest, and pavement cafes to while away an hour or so. Not feeling up to serious sightseeing we spent the morning in our room.

Before lunch I decided to venture out to see if I could buy some fruit. Met a Chinese girl in the lift. She started talking, said I could buy fruit from stalls in the street and very kindly took me to one close by. Who would have thought? Just round the corner from the hotel was a different world. Dingy shops, men on bikes, rickshaws, crowded and poor. Women in Muslim head scarves, men in Islamic hats . . . That was how I discovered that our hotel was situated next to the Muslim quarter.

Twenty minutes after leaving our room I returned with a paper bag full of peaches and oranges.

After lunch at the hotel we went by rickshaw (motorized, not man-powered, covered against the rain), to see the famous Xian Mosque. At first we held on to the side bars, but the rickshaw came dangerously close to other vehicles—cars, bikes, other rickshaws . . . We worried that we might come home minus a few fingers so we held on to the edge of our seats instead. The streets were narrow and muddy, stalls everywhere, lots of people. We were the only Westerners.

The mosque was the most beautiful and peaceful place I have ever visited, Chinese pagoda-like architecture. One courtyard after another. The entrance to each one perfectly aligned. Beautiful trees, roses and bushes with pink flowers. Quiet but for a few Chinese Muslims and the odd Western tourist. We stayed there for a long time and decided to make our way back on foot.

Things we saw: Shops that were nothing but holes in the walls. Barber shops that were nothing but dark hovels, two or three of them had one ancient decrepit chair, white enamel flaking off. In several places they were cooking white steamed buns in the street, no idea what kind of flour can be that white, rice flour perhaps. The buns tasting of nothing, yet amazingly satisfying. Four men in front of a building, one with obvious learning difficulties, one was a dwarf, all four looking desperately poor. Saw narrow and dark alleyways, only a metre or so between the houses. People selling all sorts of food stuffs, in some places boiled chickens piled high, heads and all. In one place something that looked like dried liver. Another stall sold tripe. Nice looking fruit as well. Men on rickshaws asked if we wanted a ride. We said no, wanting to make our way back on foot. In one place we heard the sound of hammering, a skinny man in late middle age was making tin washbasins. Mountains of blue duck's eggs; and some dirty-brown eggs, no idea what kind. Pavements narrow or non-existent filled with street vendors' wares. Most of the time we had to walk in the street, dodging rickshaws, bikes, cars and motorbikes. After a couple of wrong turns we saw our hotel on the corner gleaming and clean—all lights and shining marble. In front of it a street with several carriage ways and modern apartment blocks.

Good job that we hadn't gone with the rest of the group. On their return journey from the Terracotta Army the coach got stuck in gridlock and they didn't reach the hotel till after 9 by which time Maher and I had already had our dinner. They had managed a short visit to the Muslim quarter but from what they said I think they must have been taken to a section that had been sanitized for the benefit of Western tourists. They said it was nothing very special, or perhaps it is the eyes that see . . . Besides, it must have been dark by the time they finally got there.

September 10th
2009. On the boat.

Early morning scribbling by the light of my bedside lamp.

The plane landed at Wuhan Airport yesterday mid-morning. We were met by a male guide, young, round face, introduced himself as Jack, said we'd never be able to pronounce his Chinese name and that you couldn't find a shorter name than Jack. That set off the Australians: "Yes you can; Jim, Tim, Joe . . . what's shorter than Joe?" They couldn't think of anything so the game fizzled out.

The bus started. Jack did his intro about Wuhan: So and so many million people. Capital of such and such province. Lots of industry. 500 universities. Very prominent in technology and metal urge. Somebody suggested he might mean metallurgy. Lately lots of foreign visitors. His English left a lot to be desired and he often had 2—3 goes at a word before getting it reasonably right and then he'd laugh a short sharp laugh. He finished his speech by saying that he hoped we would be back in Wuhan to invest in its many industries and metal urges and that's enough for now ha-ha-ha.

We were travelling at speed through a flat landscape and as the countryside around us deepened we realised that we'd never set eyes on Wuhan and its metal urges.

Everywhere water, had to be manmade, square ponds of various sizes with a strange device in the middle. Also ponds of Lotus flowers, only a few of them in bloom, some white and some bright pink, large water lilies really. At one point gigantic bridges, a lofty spaghetti junction, almost lace-like, graceful and elegant. Part of the much talked about economic miracle that has not sifted down to the poorer parts of the population. I would have expected Jack to say something about the junction, but no.

Earlier on, when finishing his recital, Jack had asked if anyone had any questions, presumably about the industries and metal urges of Wuhan. He belonged to the type of guide we had seen on our previous visit too. Having never set foot outside China they have little concept of what seems exotic and interesting to a Westerner. Also, having been fed communist propaganda from an early age they are proud to show off their country's material accomplishments. Australian Margaret wanted to know about all the ponds.

'Fish farms.'

'And the device in the middle?'

'For oxygen.' End of story.

Somebody else wanted to know about the gigantic lily-pads.

'Lotus plants.' I could have told them that. 'People cultivate lotus plants because many people like to eat the roots, for example my daughter, ha-ha-ha.' Then silence. I drifted off to sleep, then woke up to look at the landscape. Completely flat, green, poplars. At one stage flowers along the road, looked like orange and red marigolds plus some sort of yellow lilies. Here and there a canal stretching out into the distance fading into a misty horizon. Charcoal-grey buffaloes grazing by the waterside. Where there were buffaloes also a few white ibis birds. Another canal disappearing into the mist. People working the land in cone-shaped hats. Here and there an old man tending a buffalo. Road completely straight. At intervals large boards with writing in Chinese and English: NO TIREDNING WHEN DRIVING. NO DRINKING DRIVING, etc. We stopped outside a service station for people to go to the loo. Two tiny old women were walking about with sacks, wrinkly happy faces, near toothless gums. We understood that we were meant to put any rubbish we might have in their sacks.

And so the day continued. At one stage the Australians started singing to alleviate the boredom but they soon ran out of steam. Some of us were not bored. After all, how often do you get to travel through the deep Chinese countryside?

We stopped for a meal in a town whose name I failed to register, too late for lunch and too early for dinner, but a good meal all the same.

Soon darkness was falling and Jack told us that we were nearing the place where we would be boarding the boat for our Yangtze cruise.

We turned off the main road, driving slowly through what looked like slums; the worst hovels I have ever seen. Dark and dingy holes in the cliff walls. In some of them people were selling sweets and soft drinks and things. Outside one such home people were doing exercises to a TV-programme.

Finally off the coach. Very uneven road or rather footpath. A faint street lamp here and there, far from enough to illuminate the treacherous surface full of deep holes and cracks. One unlucky step and you could easily end up with a broken ankle. Pitch dark, humid and slightly misty. Somebody, I think it was Jack, walking in front shining a torch behind him so we could watch our step. In between the trees I caught my first glimpse of the mighty Yangtze River, a shimmering, gleaming golden surface in the dark. The frogs in the bushes were laying on a tremendous concert to welcome us. I really wanted to enjoy their chorus but it was difficult because the Australians found the dodgy surface so hilarious that they couldn't stop shrieking and laughing, totally drowning out the frogs.

* * *

Cold shower at around 6am but not from choice. Turns out that the hot water on the boat doesn't come on until 7. Finally went outside.

The water of the Yangtze is muddy and brown. Two sets of very long steps leading up to the village. A few new modern blocks and more under construction. I notice a new structure that looks like the beginnings of a temple but probably isn't. A handful of individuals are sitting on the muddy riverbank with fishing rods. They will live out their lives in this corner of China whose name I'll never know, speaking no other language but their strange tongue of vowels, nasals and tones. The only sounds reminiscent of consonants are variations of the English sh or ch sounds. To think that a few generations ago a European would kill a 'Chinaman' at the drop of a hat. I once saw a horrendous photo of an Englishman standing proudly with a dozen Chinamen's heads lying on the ground. These days the Chinese are meeting out the death penalty with far greater ease than most other nations. Still the Chinese are not the only people upholding this barbaric form of punishment.

Boat still in the same place. Sugar cube mountains on both sides of the river, steep and tree-clad, shrouded in mist exactly as I have seen in innumerable photographs and tourist brochures. The yellowish-grey water sloshing against the side of the boat. Soft humid air wafting around my face. First clean air since arriving in this country. Heartfelt sigh of relief. Maher and I and a few others are scattered around the deck. No crowds on land, only the fishermen and a few hawkers. This is what I came for. I had begun to fear that the whole adventure would be a wash-out, interesting enough, but not what I had come to see—the silence and enormity of the Yangtze River. And here it is. I'm on it and this is only the beginning.

The Uncanny

Dad had a younger sister named Astrid. She was a head nurse in charge of the Unit for Internal Medicine at one of Oslo's major hospitals. She was a down-to-earth woman who never married. Belonging to a generation where few single women aspired to buying a proper house she was content to live in the nurses' block next to the hospital. Her flat was small; a fair sized bedsitter, a miniscule bathroom and a tiny kitchen plus an even tinier balcony that she scarcely used. In addition she rented two storage rooms, one in the basement and one in the attic. For years her idea of a holiday was three weeks helping out on the farm and her idea of a Sunday outing was the one hour bus-ride to visit us where she was always welcome. She only had every third or fourth Sunday off which meant that we saw her about once a month.

Auntie Astrid with my father all dressed up for the photographer,
probably in the late 1930s.
Young and full of hope. A moment in time long gone.

Auntie Astrid was a hoarder who never threw anything away, and she loved browsing in shops. In fact most of her free time was spent perusing her favourite department stores in downtown Oslo. She would scrutinize cards, pretty candles and serviettes, table mats, plates and figurines of china and glass, scarves, necklaces, rings . . . you name it. When she found something she liked, which she invariably did, she would buy it and carry it home. Because of this she seldom had to go out especially if she suddenly needed a present, there would always be something suitable in her flat, some knick-knack she had bought and never even unwrapped. In addition came all the boxes of chocolates given to her by grateful patients, which she never ate and promptly gave away, for example to us when she came to visit. In her mid-50s she took to holidaying in Spain, and so there were hankies with embroidered flamenco dancers, ashtrays decorated with shells, castanets and fans and other such souvenirs that nobody ever found use for. She always had something to give away—a piece of jewellery, a nice dish, a miniature plate with the Little Mermaid that she'd bought in Copenhagen. After moving to England I always made a point of visiting her whenever I was in Norway, or she would come to us. She was my godmother and I saw her regularly for as long as she was alive. When saying good-bye she would hand me a 500 kroner bill with the words: "Now go and buy yourself something nice." A most welcome gift as these were the years when we were struggling to make ends meet and my earnings from freelance jobs were invariably too little too late. More often than not the 500 would evaporate on clothes or treats for the boys. Still, there were times when I did buy myself something nice. Scattered about my house and in my jewellery boxes are things that originate from Auntie Astrid, one way or another.

Mum walked around the shops with her once, and only once. She had taken the bus to Oslo to buy an outfit for some occasion or other and had arranged to meet up with Astrid so they could go together. Mum's idea of a shopping expedition was to look for what she was after, find it, buy it, have lunch in her favourite café, and go home. Astrid, however, started her usual perusing, spending ages scrutinising thingamajigs, driving Mum mad as she had no interest in knick-knacks and pretty cards and was itching to get on with her day.

When Auntie Astrid passed away good old Marit was given the task of sorting out her belongings. She told me that not only was every nook and cranny in Auntie's flat stuffed full of all manner of things, the two storage rooms were also filled to the brim with every object, letter or document that had ever passed through Auntie's hands.

* * *

Out of the seven sisters and brothers in Dad's family one brother, Oluf, had settled in Canada, so his descendants were out of the equation. Her older sister, Auntie Entse, also a nurse, married but childless, had died a few years before. The remaining four, Dad included, had three children each. When everything had been tidied up and old bills and magazines and pretty carrier bags and boxes had been thrown away, the remainder was divided into four loads of roughly equal value and distributed to the off-spring of the four siblings. One of these loads, a big cartload in fact, ended up in John's garage to be shared between Dad's descendants. As Bjørn had passed away, one third of the stuff was to be split between his four sons. We all took a few things—a painting, a carved lampshade, a crystal vase. I chose a serving spoon of pewter that I remembered from my visits to Auntie's flat. She used it for serving ice cream. I also ended up with a gold ring with a large amethyst that I'm very fond of, plus a white china angel now residing on my windowsill, among other things. But the bulk was donated to our local nursing home for them to make use of or dispose of as they saw fit. Looking at the pile of hankies and serviettes with flamenco dancers, bars of pink perfumed soap that had lost their scent, necklaces of local pebbles, table mats with Christmas elves and pussycats . . . I thought to myself: Never shall I waste money on some souvenir or ornament that takes my fancy there and then, but when I get home I'll be thinking: what do I do with that? If I want something to remind me of a holiday or a good day out I'll buy an elephant to add to my collection, or a fridge magnet.

I was standing in John's garage after all of Auntie Astrid's belongings had gone when my eyes fell on a black book lying on the floor, left behind and ignored when the rest of the stuff was driven away. It was a book of sermons, old and mouldy from 50 years in a basement storage room. However, I didn't want to throw it away so I took it inside and started leafing through it. It must have belonged to my grandmother, for between the pages I found two letters from my father. One was from March 1939 and one from January 1940. My grandmother must have placed them there out of a mixture of religiousness and superstition, thinking that by putting letters from her son's hand inside a holy book she would protect him against the dangers of war. Appropriately she had placed them by the story of *the prodigal son*. I read Dad's letters and put them back where I found them and where they remained for thirteen more years until I reread them just now. That was how I discovered that most likely the photo of Dad and his friends in La Boca must have been taken in the early part of 1940.

My father survived many perils during the war, so like Mum said, there must be power in prayers. To be on the safe side I have stuck written communications from Adam and Samy in between the pages of that very same prayer book now kept safe in my bookcase, and who knows . . . Samy survived the tsunami that struck Thailand on Boxing Day 2004. He was back-packing around the world and had been spending a couple of weeks in Thailand. On Boxing Day he and some friends he'd made along the way had planned to go diving from one of the islands off the coast, but somehow they didn't get it together, and decided to go rock climbing instead. They were in the rocks above the beach when the big wave struck. The tsunami washed right over the island where they had planned to go, and as far as I know there were no survivors.

Never be too sure that there isn't more between heaven and earth than meets the eye! People who think otherwise are close-minded and block-headed, fettered to the here and now, never lifting their eyes above their everyday cares.

Letters From Afar

Here are the two letters from my father that so miraculously fell into my hands. The first one is written on proper letter-paper, folded over once, the fold is quite worn showing that it must have been read again and again. There are brown stains on it, perhaps from my grandmother's coffee. The paper has gone yellow with age but his handwriting is the same as I remember it from later years.

M/T Oregon Express. March 2nd 1939

Dear Mother.

Well, I'd better write you a few words to let you know how things are. I am now more or less well again. There is still some puss coming out of my nose, but I feel almost completely recovered and much better than I have felt for several years.

We're now on our way to San Pedro from Vancouver, Seattle and Portland. Will be arriving in a couple of hours. Perhaps you have already heard from Jonas and Hans. They arrived in Seattle on the same morning as us. And they came with Gunne-Jonas and the boys and woke me up early in the morning. Later on I was in their home and on the eve of our departure I had Jonas and Hans and most of Gunne-Jonas' family on board for coffee, and in the end I had Jonas and Hans for supper with the passengers and some guests. It was very pleasant to spend time with them as it was the first time I've met anyone from back home.

As I wrote from Europe the captain is ill. He went ashore in San Pedro on our way north and he will be back tomorrow. So I've been captaining the ship on this trip along the coast. I assume that he'll be going home when we arrive in Europe, and then it's likely I'll be in command again for a while.

Well, I suppose it must be the middle of the winter fishing season back home. I hope they'll be doing reasonably well and above all that they look after themselves out at sea.

You must give my regards to Father and Petra and everyone else. I wish I was home so that I could do something for you all. Martha writes that Bjørn has started talking quite a lot now. He will soon be coming back to see you all again. Give my regards to Maria and Aslak.

Kind regards from

Kristoffer.

Will be arriving in Le Havre around 25 March

The letter is sparse, focusing on the sort of things that his mother would relate to. Still it offers some insight into a time that's long gone.

The people he met up with were friends and neighbours from back home that had immigrated to America. The contact with that side of the family has since been lost.

The health problems he's referring to must be the operation for sinusitis. He sometimes spoke about this surgery and how he spent two weeks recuperating in a small hotel somewhere in the American countryside. I think this must have been when he stayed in the same hotel as Nordal Grieg, the legendary Norwegian poet and playwright who was shot down over Berlin in 1943. These days Nordal Grieg is best known for his heartrending poetry about the violation of our country and the loss of our freedom. Perhaps most famously for the poem *Today the flagpole stands naked among Eidsvoll's green trees* which he wrote to mark our constitution day on May 17th 1940, at the beginning of the German occupation. Eidsvoll is where the Norwegian constitution was written and signed in 1814. The Germans had forbidden any display of the Norwegian national flag, as well as any performance of our National Anthem and patriotic songs and hymns like *God bless our precious Fatherland*.

He mentions his guests' having supper with the passengers. The Oregon Express was a cargo ship and a handful of passengers were obviously part of the routine. Officers and passengers would sit up into the night, sipping drinks and telling anecdotes from their fascinating lives, or so I assumed, romantic as I was.

My father's stories became such a part of me that I took it for granted that I too would see the world and meet the sort of people he'd been hanging out with. An ordinary life in the place I was born was simply not on my agenda. In my youth I did manage to do some travel; I had visited a penfriend in Scotland and I had made my way by ferry to Copenhagen and from there by train to Paris where I worked as an au pair to perfect my French. The family had a summer house in Normandy, so I got to spend time in the countryside of 'la Douce France' as well. Finally, I travelled down to San Remo, by train to Nice, and then on the back of the motorbike of a Canadian girl I had met at the youth hostel where I stayed. I was on my way, or so I believed.

There are many psychological reasons why we marry as we do but I shan't go into them here. Suffice to say that Maher, an Egyptian scientist with a one year scholarship to Norway, seemed like the personification of everything I had dreamed of. He was handsome, not very tall, only a couple of inches taller than me, causing me to stop wearing high heels. He drank tea from a glass and thick black coffee from tiny cops and used an aftershave that smelt of lemons. He glowed with sun of the Orient, and out of all the girls hanging around him he preferred me who, by Norwegian standards, was not very special. Blond (in a country where half the population is fair-haired), under average height. Not very confident, not very sporty, qualities that were highly praised in 1970s Norway and probably still are. I was studious, preferring books to partying, and forever dreaming of a life less ordinary. And, actually; I wasn't hanging around him.

Then followed our move to London—the shock of discovering a standard of living much lower than what I'd been used to and taken for granted. Money remained tight for years and any travel abroad, apart from our yearly holiday in Norway, was out of the question.

Our first vacation further afield was a packet holiday to Corfu. Picture my disappointment upon discovering that our companions were ordinary working folk from Yorkshire. Kind and decent, but poets and countesses they were not. The world had changed; travelling to exotic locations was nothing special any more.

Back to Dad's letter: He mentions Petra who was his youngest sister, named after his mother, and Maria and Aslak. Maria was the sister who did not become a nurse and the mother of my friend, Marit. Aslak was her husband. Marit succumbed to cancer three years ago but I'm Facebook friends with her youngest daughter, Hanne Marie, now in her late 30s. We are both keen photographers and enjoy sharing our photos on Facebook where we "like" and comment on each other's work.

Whether Dad made it to Norway during the summer of 1939 and took Bjørn to see his family in the West Country I shall never know. I only have the two letters from the prayer book; plus a few telegrams that John found in the attic. People communicated by telegram back then—a medium made obsolete by the advent of cheap international phone-calls.

* * *

The second letter is dated nearly a year later. It's written on lined A4 paper, yellow with age and with one large stain, same evidence of having been passed from hand to hand and read and reread. By then he was in command of the Herbrand who was to remain his ship for part of the war.

M/T Herbrand January 8th 1940

Dear Mother.

Long time now since I wrote to you. Actually it doesn't much matter to which one of you I address my letters and I haven't really got a lot to write about either.

I had a letter from Anders in our last harbour but apart from that I haven't heard from Norway for 4 months. Anders wrote that everything is well back home, but he was sad because he hadn't got to go whaling. (Anders was his cousin and when mentioning whaling he is probably referring to the southern seas. Even if my father can't have enjoyed whale hunting he doesn't seem to have seen anything wrong in it, and it was good money.) We are now on our way to Buenos Aires and will arrive in 3—4 days. We are lucky to have this run. We hardly notice the war at all and we mostly have good weather. I still haven't heard from the shipping company as regards to how long I'll remain here. We'll be making one tour to Coveñas (Colombia) and back to Buenos Aires and after that we'll go to Galveston for docking, as far as I know. If the old skipper is returning at all, it is likely that he'll be arriving then. That will be at the beginning of April, and if he takes over I should be back home in the month of May. But I don't know anything for certain and it is quite possible that I'll be continuing this run for a while. However, there is no denying that I would like to come home but it's out of my hands. I was hoping that I would manage to save up enough money to start something back home, but in these uncertain times one can't count on anything.

Apart from this I don't seem to have much to write about. Soon it will be time for people back home to think of the winter fishing season. I hope they'll be in luck. I can hardly believe that it's already 14 years since I last went fishing.

Say hello to Father and Petra and everyone else from me. I hope that before long we'll be seeing each other again.

Kind regards

Kristoffer

Little did he know of the horrors to come and that it would take more than six years before he would see his family again. Here are some of the telegrams that he sent home before he next set foot in Norway. John found them in a brown envelope in the attic.

On December 23rd 1939 he sends the following telegram from the Herbrand to my mother: *Wishing you and Bjørn and everyone back home a pleasant Christmas, hopefully we will be celebrating next Christmas together. Loving regards, Kristoffer*

Herbrand March 17th 1940 to Martha Hoddevik: *Send me a telegram to let me know if you have received parcel sent from Buenos Aires. Greetings to you both, Kristoffer*

Then nothing till after the war which seems to confirm that there was little or no communication with occupied Norway during those years.

Herbrand July 21st 1945, this time in English. The other telegrams were in Norwegian: *Thanks for telegrams and letters. Cannot say when coming home. Regards to all. Love Kristoffer*

Herbrand March 10th 1946 to Bjørn Hoddevik: *Happy birthday. Hope you'll have a pleasant party. Regards to you and Mum. From Dad*

Bjørn was born on the 12th of March 1937 and would have been nine years old.

Herbrand May 8th 1946 to Martha Hoddevik: *Expecting to arrive in Rotterdam on May 17th. Coming home from there. Regards to you and Bjørn. Kristoffer*

I've always been under the impression that he returned in autumn, but I may have been wrong.

Background

The Battle of the Atlantic, the Blitz on Liverpool

The Battle of the Atlantic was the longest running campaign of the Second World War and began with the sinking of the passenger liner SS Athenia on 3 September 1939. The capabilities of the U-boats were demonstrated very soon after the outbreak of war when the Royal Navy's main port at Scapa Flow, off the Orkney Islands, had been infiltrated and the HMS Royal Oak was sunk with the loss of 830 lives. With the fall of France and Norway in the summer of 1940 the U-boat became a great threat. The German air force was able to use air bases in Europe to locate the convoys and direct the U-boats to them.

Commercial ships were under threat from surface raiders and bombing from aircraft. However, the biggest threat was the German submarines. The main countermeasure to this threat was the reintroduction of the convoy system, where large groups of merchant vessels, from 20 to 100, sailed together in ordered formation and were protected by naval ships. Each convoy was led by a commodore who was stationed on board one of the ships. He had the overview of the convoy, communicated with the captains and was responsible for steering the ships towards the destination. At the start of a crossing the captains would be ordered to rendezvous at a certain departure point, for example a large expanse of calm water: outside Liverpool, in Scapa Flow, or Belfast Lough, to mention three. There they would take their allotted place in the formation and set sail for their destination.

After the fall of France in June 1940 the Germans were able to use the French Atlantic ports as bases. This allowed U-boats to reach far out into the Atlantic and the Mediterranean for the first time. Germany soon began to wage unrestricted U-boat warfare around the coast of Britain and out into the Atlantic. In 1940 the Norwegian vessels were unarmed, but slowly defensive measures like guns to attack surfaced submarines and low-flying aircraft were added.

For the first time, small U-boats 'pack attacks' were used, with devastating effect, against the still largely unprotected British convoys. By late October 1940 the Admiralty feared that the U-boats were close to victory in the Atlantic.

In 1939 the German Navy (Kriegsmarine) was not strong enough to risk a major battle with the Royal Navy, which was still the largest navy in the world. Instead, the German aim was to defeat Britain by ruthlessly attacking her merchant ships and those of any other country which supported her. This long and bitter campaign was fought worldwide, but was at its most relentless in the North Atlantic. The Germans used U-boats, mines, surface warships and aircraft. As in the First World War, however, the U-boats posed the deadliest threat to Britain's survival.

However, the result of new tactics, intelligence and aircraft saw the German Navy suffering heavy losses, and by May 1943 the U-boats were called off by the German Naval Command. Although the battle did not end there, the threat of the U-boat had greatly decreased. The campaign resulted in high casualties on both sides, and it is estimated that some 80,000 Allied seamen were lost, while some 28,000 out of 41,000 U-boat crews were also lost. 12.8 million tons of Allied and neutral shipping were destroyed.

Winston Churchill was later to state: 'The Battle of the Atlantic was the dominating factor all through the war. Never for one moment could we forget that everything happening elsewhere, on land, at sea or in the air depended ultimately on its outcome.'

The Blitz on Liverpool

*T*he blitz on London is well known and publicized. The Blitz on Liverpool rather less so. Liverpool was targeted by the Germans and badly hit because it was Europe's main port, vital for the Allied war effort. Troops, fuel, weapons and food all came through Liverpool, brought in by the convoys that crossed the Atlantic incessantly, a great number of ships perishing on the way. The convoys were controlled from a command centre beneath a 1930s office building and the supplies they brought in to Liverpool saved Britain and made the Liberation of Europe possible.

The Luftwaffe launched sixty-eight bombing raids on Merseyside between July 1940 and January 1942. The worst of these occurred during "The May Blitz" of 1941 in which very heavy raids occurred on each of the first seven nights of the month: 2,315 high explosive bombs and 119 other explosives such as incendiaries. 1,741 people were killed and 1,154 injured. Also 18 British merchant ships of 35,605 tons were sunk and 25 other ships of altogether 92,964 tons were badly damaged. 69 out of 144 cargo docks were destroyed and the turnover capacity of the port was reduced to one quarter.

The Liverpool Blitz brought the Battle of the Atlantic home to everyone on Merseyside. Although the docks were the main targets, enormous damage was caused to the city and residential areas on both sides of the river Mersey. In all some 4,000 people were killed and another 4,000 seriously injured. 10,000 homes were completely destroyed and 184,000 damaged. Probably the heaviest loss per head of population of any British city. Yet the Liverpool Blitz remains the forgotten Blitz. It is still thought that raids on Liverpool were not publicised in the hope of concealing their accuracy and effectiveness from the Germans.

How did the German bombers make it all the way to Liverpool? They were long range bombers, starting out from occupied France. They did not fly in a straight line to Liverpool. Instead they would fly across the English Channel to St David's Head on the Bristol Channel, then north to Cardigan Bay and then east-north-east over Anglesey towards Liverpool. This route was clear of anti-aircraft defences and the pilots could use the lights of Dublin to guide them as the Irish Republic was neutral and therefore had no black-out.

In Harbour but far from safe

Ships loaded with oil or ammunition were prime targets.

My father's ship, the Herbrand, was a 14,750 tonne oil tanker built in Copenhagen in 1935. She was in Port Arthur, Texas, when Norway was invaded by the Germans on April 9th 1940, having arrived there from Beaumont (most likely Canada) on April 8th. She left again for Trinidad on April 11th. As far as I have been able to establish, she spent the first year of the war mainly sailing the Caribbean. Further records indicate that she spent quite a long time in New York in 1941, having arrived there from Boston on June 16th. The departure date is given as August 25th when she headed for Halifax in order to join Convoy HX 148 to the UK along with the Norwegian Ørnefjell.

According to records Herbrand spent 1941-44 mainly in convoys between the USA and the UK, very often with Liverpool as final destination. However, my father was only in charge of the Herbrand until late 1942. The records that can be found on the Internet are not complete. Several voyages are missing during which the Herbrand could have gone anywhere, for example to Murmansk.

There is a small possibility that the Herbrand was anchored in Liverpool for a day or two during that terrible week of May 1st 1941, but it is unlikely. The window during which she could have made the crossings to Europe and back seems too short. I have been unable to establish her whereabouts before arriving in Boston on June 16th, so there is a chance that she was in Liverpool, but that's only speculation. As the bombing of Merseyside was on-going, all-be-it less intense, and as the Herbrand made two documented dockings in Liverpool during 1941-42, possibly more, chances are that my father must have seen some of the action. The records indicate nothing about who was captaining the ship, but my father saw the Herbrand as 'his' ship so it's fair to assume that where the Herbrand went from April 1940 to late 1942, my father went too. During this period she made at least eight North Atlantic crossings, four of them Halifax—Liverpool and back. On May 7th the Herbrand sailed from Aruba to Freetown, Sierra Leone, and from Freetown to Clyde near Newcastle where she arrived on June 22nd. There were also voyages between Halifax and Guantanamo. There must have been other voyages too, but as I said, the records have gaps.

* * *

More than seventy years have gone by since my father docked in Liverpool during World War II. Enough time for a person to be born, grow up, find his way in life and retire. That's how long has passed since Captain Kristoffer Hoddevik sailed up the Mersey having miraculously avoided being hit by a German torpedo, bombed by a German plane or shot at from a German warship. After the perils of the Atlantic he would have made his way up the flat and peaceful estuary and continued up the wide and shallow Mersey, even and calm like a millpond. A huge sigh of relief as he saw the Liver Birds on top of the Royal Liver Building, the fabled birds that don't look like real birds and have been guarding Liverpool since 1911. Legend has it that if the birds fly away Liverpool will cease to exist, which may explain why they are tethered to their towers by thick chains.

Finally safe from the marauding U-boats and war ships of the German Wehrmacht, but not from their bomber planes. And the evidence of the bombing is everywhere. Venture ashore and all you see is rubble. Warehouses and factories along the port have been bombed, walls sticking up like broken teeth in a ravaged mouth. Further inland whole buildings and entire blocks have been erased; a battered sofa here, a crushed car there. Broken bricks and dust and the memories of people who once lived there. Eerie silence on the nights when no bombs are falling, rats and homeless souls rummaging through the rubble.

Safe from the German U-boats, but not from their planes. Waves of terrifying planes coming in at night, concentrating on the harbour, a hell of thunder and fire. The whole area shaking and burning. Fire and debris raining down from the sky. Men, women and children running for shelter. There is a story of a drunk man seeing horses escaping from a bombed-out brewery declaring: "Look, they're even dropping horses!" The crew of the Herbrand on shore leave. God knows exactly where. Resting in the arms of a woman perhaps, or drinking in some harbour-side pub. It's what they need after days and nights on the open ocean expecting to be blown to smithereens at any moment. Staggering to the nearest shelter with the rest of the clientele grabbing their drinks as they run.

Captain Kristoffer Hoddevik remained on his ship, and if the Captain was staying so were the Chief, i.e. the First Engineer, and the First and Second Officers. They had all been ashore, had a glass or two with the men, but it didn't do for officers to fraternize with ordinary seamen, to become too familiar. So the officers stayed with their Captain on the bridge, hearing the roar of bombs and watching buildings turn into flames, sending towers of smoke and sparks into the sky, as they had watched ships explode in flames, burn and be gone, out on the open Atlantic.

People back in Norway did their bit too. Suddenly and without introduction Jan Tollefsen, the First Officer, started telling a story, almost a legend that had done the rounds of Norwegian ships and sailors' bars, and more elevated circles as well. Kristoffer found it especially interesting because it had happened close to where Martha and Bjørn live, on a stretch where the road from Oslo descends in sharp bends towards the lake, with a sheer cliff on one side and a hundred metre drop on the other. Kristoffer knew it well. This is what happened: An ordinary Norwegian bus-driver had been made to drive a busload of German soldiers. When he came to the section with the cliff on one side and the drop on the other, he suddenly speeded up and before the Germans could even think or do anything he had driven the bus over the edge and straight into the abyss. The Germans all perished, as did the driver. He had sacrificed his life and because of that some 30 German soldiers were gone from the earth. Kristoffer had heard this story many times before and so had the others, but they let Tollefsen tell it all the same. It took his mind off the bombs that were raining down around them. If Kristoffer ever got back to Norway he would ask Martha about it, perhaps she or someone in her family had even known the driver.

The Chief was the first to spot it—he would. His keen brown eyes everywhere, seeing everything, a God send this chief, nothing would get

70

past him and his men feared him and respected him even though he was younger than many of them. Right now he nudged the other three and pointed towards a building with a flat roof. In the flickering light of surrounding fires they could see men, running around on the roof grasping and chucking incendiary bombs off the roof as they landed. Down on the ground were other men smothering the bombs in sand. Captain Hoddevik and his officers forgot about the exploding houses and watched mesmerized as the men ran around continuing their desperate fight against the incendiaries. They had heard about this type of bravery but never witnessed it. Rumour had it that in Moscow Stalin put 15-16 year-olds up on the roofs of the wooden houses to immerse the incendiaries in water as they landed.

Then the sky grew quiet. Only one explosion further down the docks as a German bomber dropped its last bomb. Soon after the all clear sounded. The First Officer remained on duty on the Bridge but the Captain and the others walked the few steps to their quarters. The whole spectacle had lasted less than an hour and a half but for those who had lived through it, it felt more like five or six, like the world could never be the same again. Perhaps worst of all was the knowledge that during that one hour God knows how many people had died or lost their homes.

Back in his quarters the Captain poured himself a stiff whisky. He never knocked himself out with alcohol when out at sea, but off duty, in harbour, he sometimes did. His legs ached. Some of the larger veins were much too prominent, like knotted ropes under the skin. But what could you expect? You don't stand on the Bridge for three days and nights in a row without repercussions. Standing still, keeping an ever watchful eye out for signs of German subs. Tiredness coming and going in waves, like a vice tightening around his forehead. He needed to sleep and sleep, but how? Each time he put his head down, he was wide awake, seeing ships exploding in a ball of fire.

He topped up his glass, put *La Comparasita* on his wind-up record player, sank down onto his brown leather armchair, leaned back and closed his eyes taking another large sip of the whisky. Yet again he had made it. He was alive, at least for now. The seductive tango rhythms of *La Comparasita*—he'd bought the record in Buenos Aires after hearing it in a restaurant. It must have been in La Cabaña when the Chief had wanted to impress with his ten Spanish words and had ordered far too much food and they had struggled to finish it, delicious though it was . . . The sound quality was screechy and none too good, as if travelling through space from distant lands to this hell hole of a city. The tango filled his cabin, conjuring up a world where music flowed and lovely women danced and were happy—laughing, drinking, not a care in the world. His wife, Martha, cropped up in his mind. He didn't think of her often. More and more she was turning into a faded memory, a beautiful young woman with dark brown eyes and black hair. Last time he saw her there were already streaks of grey in it, even though she was only 28. When they went to a Jewish photographer in Oslo, the photographer let them have the photos nearly for free because he thought she was Jewish, and may-be he was right, Martha's whole family looks dark and different, and she has no idea where her grandparents came from. His family adored her—Kristoffer's beautiful bride from the East Country. No news from his family, no news from anyone, only rumours of food shortages and German brutality in occupied Norway, and he was here. *La Comparasita* had finished playing. He wound up the gramophone and started the record again, poured himself another drink. His family had the farm; surely they would manage to keep a lamb away from the hands of the marauding Germans, hide potatoes in the barn. Apparently that was how they ruled the country, forcing farmers and smallholders to hand over their produce and penalizing them if they failed to comply, thus leaving people with little or nothing to eat, reducing them to scavenge for food, eating thrushes and plants they would never look at in peace time, taking the food from the mouths of hungry Norwegians to sustain them in their quest for world domination: 'Lebensraum für Deutschland' the God-given right of the master race. Their fiendish philosophy wreaking havoc around the whole world! Yes, that was it, salt down a lamb and hide potatoes and carrots in the barn. His parents were smart; surely they'd think of that. Potatoes and carrots, good food, and fish of course, plenty of fish in the sea . . . He woke up from something cold running down his trouser-leg, the whisky; he had fallen asleep with the glass in his hand. He set it down, stripped off his clothes and dived into bed, tonight he would sleep; he knew it, and tomorrow—another crossing.

A Long
January Night

Dark now. Convoy forging ahead, dark, dark, dark. No lights to be seen. Ships painted grey for camouflage. Total blackout. One 50 Watt light bulb can be spotted a mile off. Alone on the Bridge but for the Second Officer and an able seaman at the helm, worried about him. He had drunk heavily in Liverpool, more heavily than before. Nerves getting the better of them all. Wind raising, screaming, roaring. Towering white-crested waves crashing over the deck. Ship staying afloat all the same, taking a nose dive, then righting itself, rolling over to one side, then levelling out. Waves don't frighten him. They've been a constant presence in his life, watching them as a child, sailing on them for more than twenty-five years. The Herbrand is solid; she'll ride out the storm, no problem at all. What does frighten him is what's lurking below the surface—the German submarines. Still no sign of them. For now, only the sea, but it won't last. Submarines will attack, if not tonight, then tomorrow morning or tomorrow night or the day after. Open Atlantic for days ahead. The subs will find the convoy, always do, like a pack of wolves smelling their pray. Always. Never peace. They often attack at night.

Captain Kristoffer Hoddevik looks at his wristwatch in the glow of the radar screen. One minute past midnight. Good watch this, been ticking away for 25 years. Confirmation present. Gold. Father must have saved hard to buy it for him. Many mouths to feed, new mouth every 2—3 years. Mother looking tired, big stomach whether pregnant or not. Fishing often going wrong, fish not always where you expect it to be. But Father got him a gold watch for his confirmation, and a dark-grey suit, his first, didn't last long, soon too small, still good as new. Brother Oluf had it for his confirmation two years later, that and a brand new gold watch. How did Father do it? And send the girls away to school. That was after Kristoffer left. Most girls finished elementary school in the village and stayed at home helping on the farm till they married a local fisherman/farmer or went into service. Not his sisters. Last time he heard from home Entse was already a qualified nurse, Astrid was doing her training and little Petra was set to follow. Four minutes past midnight. Still no sign of the enemy. Perhaps he could rest his legs for a while, grab the chance while it's there. No rest if the subs start attacking. He could feel them in his bones. They were out there, a pack of underwater wolves, on the prowl, ready for the kill. Impossible to see the periscope in the dark. Impossible to see the torpedo trail, a line of froth on the surface, among the roaring towering waves. They will attack, he knows it, feels it, stronger than ever before. Ship's engine humming away, nicely, perfectly. Chief on duty tonight, down in the engine room doing his best. A God send this chief, signed on just over three weeks ago, in New York, young but he has what it takes. His men look up to him. The former chief went mad, mad as a hatter. Who can blame him? Not everyone can take the pressure, days on end knowing that this minute might be your last. The trick is not to dwell on it, but even so. He knew the chief was in trouble when he stopped washing and shaving. That's always a sure sign. Then he locked himself in his cabin, eating chocolates. Where on earth had he got hold of so many boxes of chocolates? 'Open the door!' Kristoffer had called to him whilst banging hard on his door. And to his surprise the Chief had come to the door and opened it. Filthy pyjamas, not bothering to cover up his modesty, then he slumped back on his berth, stuffing another chocolate into his mouth, his face suddenly distorted with fury, spitting out the chocolate with great force landing it in a corner with a pile of other unwanted chocolates, all with a nut in the centre as far as Kristoffer could make out. 'A fucking hard one!' he shouted, 'they know I can't stand the hard ones, so why do they keep giving them to me! They're trying to break me, that's why, trying to get me to crack, but I won't!' he shouted, 'do you hear me, it's no good trying to bribe me, I'm telling you, I know you're working for Hitler, but it's no good. I'll never crack, do you hear! You may as well leave! Just go, right now! Go!' Kristoffer left the cabin, quietly securing the lock from the outside, you couldn't risk a mad man running around, wreaking havoc on board, whereupon he telegraphed the office in in New York that they had a crazy man on board needing urgent hospitalisation, possibly restraining as soon as they arrived, if they arrived. Very sad, the man had a wife and three children. In hospital he would be safe, and perhaps even recover.

The new Chief is unique. One of five survivors from a cargo ship that had been sunk in mid Atlantic. One of the lucky ones to be picked up by an escort vessel. Most men were not so lucky, he had seen them, struggling to stay afloat in the water. Men like burning torches jumping into the sea from stricken tankers, only the sea was burning too, an ocean of flames. No surviving anywhere. But Chief had survived one hour in the sea, the red lights on his life jacket spotted by someone on one of the destroyers escorting his convoy as he bobbed up and down in the water. Lead in his boots to keep him upright, rubber suit to preserve his body heat. Little red lights on the shoulders ... Kristoffer could take anything but the little red lights of the men in the sea. The order was non-negotiable: Never stop to pick up survivors. Change course to avoid them and you might cause a collision resulting in further loss of life without saving the men in the water. Convoy must keep going, a ship slowing down or stopping is an easier target and can cause collision, ship and men destroyed for no good purpose. Keep going, keep forging ahead, 80 meters behind the ship in front of you, slightly less distance to the ships on either side. This convoy had six columns, each column had nine ships. 54 ships in all when the convoy assembled at Belfast Lough. The Herbrand, no. 3 from the front, second column from port. At least he wasn't on the flank. The red lights ... The Herbrand had once ploughed straight into a cluster of red lights. What could he do? They were in the way. "Don't change course to avoid survivors in the sea." He had ploughed straight into them. It was dark so he hadn't seen the water turning red, but knowing about the blood-red water had created an image in his head that was there to stay. But it hadn't always been dark and that was far worse: Desperate men in the sea. He could see their faces, features distorted with fear and desperation, waving at the passing ship, screaming to be saved. But the order was clear: "Don't stop to pick up survivors". And then the final act of desperation, swimming away from the passing ship not to get pulled into the backwash. Some got away gaining another few minutes of life. But, where there is life there is hope and some men really did get picked up by an escorting vessel. Others who did not manage to escape got sucked into the back-sweep and into the propellers, turning the water in the wake of the ship into frothy pink foam. Kristoffer had seen it in spite of trying to avert his eyes, and the sight would remain with him forever.

Many of his men slept in their wetsuits in case they suddenly had to jump into the water. Kristoffer didn't wear his. It was too sweaty and uncomfortable. Also, if it got torn during evacuation it would fill up with water and you'd sink like a stone so there was no guarantee that it would save your life. If your number is up it's up, that's all there is to it. No use panicking because tomorrow you might be dead. It would only serve one purpose—to unsettle himself and his men and weaken his judgement and authority. A frightened captain is worse than no captain at all.

Still no sign of the enemy. Kristoffer entered the little alcove off the bridge and sat down in what was intended to be a comfortable chair but wasn't really. His legs were aching. Feet aching. It would be a long night. Long day ahead and long night after that if he lived that long. Impossible to know. But for now calm. He'd sit down for a while, rest his legs . . .

His little boy in Norway came into his mind. Martha had named him Bjørn without consulting him, just presented him with the name as a fait accompli. He hadn't even been at his son's christening. He'd been en route to the Far East, possibly passing through the Suez Canal. Hadn't seen the boy since he was two. Born in 1937 he'd be four already. Brown eyes, yellow hair, but most likely his hair had turned brown by now. Children with blond hair and brown eyes seldom stay blond for long. The boy took after his mother, nothing from him or his family. If he survived the war, there would be money, lots of money, money for risking his life every day for however long this nightmare would last.

My mother and Bjørn, eight months old

76

When Nortraship took over the Norwegian merchant fleet and they started sailing under British administration a problem arose. Norwegian sailors were better paid than their British counterparts, mainly due to receiving a higher "war hazard pay" for sailing in dangerous waters, and these days every water was dangerous, the Atlantic, the Pacific, the Mediterranean, the Indian Ocean ... The enemy was omnipresent. The British exerted pressure to make this hazard pay equivalent to that of British sailors. After negotiations with Nortraship in London in the summer of 1940 it was agreed that the difference would be paid into a special account, thereby reducing the salary of the Norwegians. The Norwegian sailors accepted this with the understanding that they would get the money owed to them after the war. Still, it was a bitter blow; a cut in salary for risking your life every day! They sailed to help their country, but still ... Don't worry, the Nortraship bosses had told them. Your money will be put in trust for you and you'll receive it when the war is over. The sailors found this reasonable, good even. When they spent their pay on women and booze they did so with an easy heart, thinking that as long as they were sailing and their ship kept afloat, money would be mounting up in the bank, slowly but surely. If they died the money would stop, which was fair enough, but whatever had been amassed in their names would be given to their families and be a good help for them. Kristoffer certainly wasn't in it for the money, none of them were. All the same it was good to know that when this madness was over they would be rewarded for their effort and for constantly risking their lives.

Unbelievably the money would also stop if their ships were sunk and they had to go in the life boats. They didn't get paid for being in a life boat. Sitting in an open boat in rain and storm, starving and getting frostbite was seen as a holiday. Kristoffer's friend from the Sea Academy, Johan, had lost both legs due to frostbite in the Arctic Sea after four days in a life boat. His legs had to be amputated in a hospital in Murmansk. At least he's out of it. God knows where he is now, languishing in the home of his old parents most likely, or perhaps he had a wife who is non-too pleased to be married to an invalid, but trying to put on a brave face ... who knows.

Kristoffer thinks of the money, something solid to look forward to, a savings-account really. All in all a hefty sum waiting for him, as he hardly spends any of his salary. Fraternising with his men, drinking and womanizing in harbours is a definite no-no for a Captain. Apart from that there isn't much on which to spend money. He does understand the men though, what other relief is there after weeks at sea knowing that you could be blown to smithereens any minute. Anyway, boozing doesn't interest him. If he gets home he'll build a house for himself and his family, an impressive house with balconies and turrets, black shiny roof tiles like he's seen on grand old houses in Oslo—a house to be passed down through the generations. Passers-by will look at the house and ask: 'Who lives there?' 'It's Captain Hoddevik. He was out at sea all through the war and built that house with money he'd saved up.' There might even be enough left over to send Bjørn to boarding school in England. That would set him up for life, make a gentleman out of him ... a naval officer perhaps, like the commodore of this convoy. Kristoffer has only met him once, at the office in Liverpool; tall and slim, an ageing English admiral and gentleman with aristocratic ancestry written all over him. The son of Kristoffer from the West Country—an English gentleman, yeah, that would be it ... out of bad comes good. Some good must come out of this madness.

He rested his head against the back of his chair and closed his eyes. Wind howling, waves lashing, the voices of the dead whispering, moaning, filling the air around him. A fête in his village school. Everybody was there, even Granny who'd passed away two years ago. She looked her old self, bossy and fat, wasn't interested in talking or hearing anyone's news even though she'd been dead for two years. She'd hoisted the Norwegian flag high above her house. Weird, he'd never noticed that she had a flagpole. Kristoffer was supposed to arrange tables and chairs in the school but he had forgotten about it and now everybody was arriving, red lights on their shoulders. A ship had been sunk outside the village and the survivors had swum ashore. Flowers on the tables! He was supposed to have put flowers on the tables! But where would he find flowers? He'd have to run home and get his mother's pot plants, but where was the road? No road leading from the school house, only choppy sea, blood red with pink frothy waves.

The roar of a huge explosion jerked him out of his dream. He jumped up, bounded onto the bridge. The tanker next to them on the port side was on fire, belching flames and black smoke. The nightmare of his dream turning into the nightmare of reality. The rumbling boom of depth charges. One of the escort ships must have managed to locate a submarine.

Another almighty bang and the orange lights of a gigantic fire lit up the sky. He couldn't see the stricken ship. It must be behind them somewhere.

Also, it must be an empty tanker, like his. Tankers were dangerous even when empty. It was impossible to empty out the oil tanks completely. A few drops, quite a lot really, would always be left on the bottom, and gass would develop, if the ship got hit, the gass would explode, and boom, into the air you went. In the flickering light the Captain could see the hands on his watch. Only 12.23. An endless night lay ahead, if he lived.

Background

The Arctic Convoys

*B*etween June 1941 and May 1945 one in every 20 Allied ships (104 in all) sailing in convoys to and from North Russia was sunk. The cost of the Russian convoys to the Royal Navy was also high (22 ships) and included the sinking of the cruisers Edinburgh and Trinidad. The German navy lost four surface warships and 31 U-boats. On both sides casualties among crews were often higher than in the Atlantic due to the appallingly cold Arctic winter.

The route to the Northern Soviet ports was around occupied Norway and therefore particularly dangerous due to the proximity of German air, submarine and surface forces. There was also the likelihood of severe weather, the frequency of fog, strong currents and drift ice.

In July 1942, the Arctic convoys suffered a significant defeat when Convoy **PQ 17** lost 24 of its 35 merchant ships during a series of heavy enemy daylight attacks which lasted a week. On the 27th of June, the ships sailed eastbound from Hvalfjord, Iceland, for the port of Arkhangelsk. The convoy was located by German forces on the 1st of July, after which it was shadowed continuously and attacked. The convoy's progress was being observed by the British Admiralty, which ordered the ships to scatter because of information that German navy surface units were being refuelled to intercept the convoy.

Two months later, in September 1942 another strongly protected convoy **PQ18** lost one third of its merchant ships (13 out of 39) to German aircraft and U-boats. The main damage to both convoys had been caused by aircraft. The switching of many of these aircraft to other theatres of war led to much lighter losses in other Arctic convoys.

Where Hell
Freezes Over

When reading about the Arctic convoys I'm shocked that there is no mention of Norwegian ships or other Allied ships that were sunk. It is as though they never existed. Why have they been so forgotten? The Norwegian ships sailed under British command but they still belonged to another nation without which the Allies could not have defeated the Germans, so why have they been so shamefully ignored?

The very mention of Arctic Convoys was enough to strike dread into a sailor's heart. There were stories. The borders between fact and hear-say were blurred.

Because of the extreme weather conditions the Arctic convoys were considered the most dangerous of all. Wild stormy seas. High waves washing over the deck instantly turning to ice in winter. Ice gathering on decks, ropes and railings. Seamen hacking away at it with axes to stop it from growing too thick and heavy, weighing down the ship till it sank. In winter, perpetual dark. In summer, endless daylight. No such thing as "under cover of darkness". Ships being stricken, men in life boats, unable to survive for long in the extreme cold. And all the while pounded by aircraft from above, U-boats from below and warships from the surface. One of the world's most hostile environments made worse by man's evil intent. I knew it was bad but I didn't realise how bad until I saw Jonathan Dimbleby's wonderful programme series about Russia which includes scenes from the Murmansk run.

And when they finally made it to Murmansk . . . The combination of Stalin's brutal regime . . . food supplies initially reduced because of the disastrous effects of the collectivisation of agriculture . . . the horror of Stalin's purges in the 1930s and now the added hardships of fighting the Germans. Add to that the harsh climate and desolate landscape of the far North, and you have the recipe for what must have been one of the bleakest and most terrifying places on earth. In his novel *We, the Drowned* the Danish author, Carsten Jensen, writes that the harbour labourers were prisoners kept in check by women who did not hesitate to shoot a prisoner scrambling for a piece of food. The novel is well researched so I tend to believe that this is true. It stands to reason as most able-bodied Soviet men had been called up to fight Hitler on more southern fronts like Stalingrad. So, for the sailors who had finally made it through to Murmansk or Archangel . . . no respite in harbour bars or in the arms of women, very likely they were not allowed shore leave at all. Strangely my father never spoke of it. Was it because he wished to put it all behind him or because he thought we wouldn't be interested or wouldn't understand?

As youngsters we were under the impression that my father had made several or at least three trips to Murmansk, although he never specified this in so many words, and as always, we didn't think to ask. He hated the Murmansk run most of all. I remember him telling us that once he overheard one of his men saying: 'I just heard the Captain swearing. That means we're going to Murmansk'. Otherwise he never swore.

We knew the main facts about his life during the War. We knew that he had sailed in convoys, that he was one of the youngest but also one of the best if not **the** best skipper in the Norwegian commercial fleet. The fact that his ship often served as escort oiler seems to substantiate this. An escort oiler was a tanker that supplied fuel to the escorting warships, a highly dangerous operation as it required both ships to be stationary during the process, which greatly increased their chances of being attacked. There were other captains in other convoys whose ships were escort oilers too, and no doubt equally brave and competent. We knew that the German wolf packs, as their clusters of tiny U-boats were called, were merciless once they had located a convoy and like wolves did not give up on their prey but kept attacking, consigning one ship after the other to smoke and flames. We knew that my father would remain on the bridge for three nights and days in a row without a break and that he developed varicose veins in his legs as a result. His crew referred to him as the Iron Man, but of course he was not the only one. The sailors all lived through hell and that's the long and short of it. Still, we knew or had the impression that somehow he was in a class of his own. Somewhere along the line he must have gone through a pain barrier, physical and emotional, which we believed was why ordinary day to day matters were of little interest to him. We assumed that he had seen action at sea, but had no idea where and how because he never spoke about it except for the episode when a sudden storm concealed him from a German warship off the coast of South or Central America. Till his dying day he believed that this was divine intervention, and very likely it was.

In short, we were not ignorant of his contributions to the Allied war effort. However, we did not comprehend or see the full extent of his experiences. I mean the horror of seeing the tanker next to yours receiving a direct hit, belching flames and black smoke. The awfulness of watching men on fire jumping into the water, which was also on fire, due to the burning oil. And, knowing that your ship could be next and that there wasn't a thing you could do to prevent it. During the day and in relatively calm weather you could see the frothy torpedo trail and if spotted in time there was a chance you might steer clear of the torpedo, only to see it hitting another ship instead of yours. The ships transporting ammunition such as nitroglycerine were the most hazardous and were referred to as suicide ships. One hit and all that remained was a sky-high column of flames. Could anything compare to the horror of steering right through a cluster of little red lights at night? But the order was clear: "Don't stop to pick up survivors". The escort ships would pick them up when possible, but there was a limit to how many they had room for. Also, they sometimes got hit in the process.

Then there were the storms and if not storms, the fog, so thick that ships collided because of lack of visibility. In clear weather the planes and surface ships were having a field day. My father was not the only one to go through a pain barrier, some men went crazy, many were damaged for life, physically or mentally or both.

No, we did not have full understanding of any of this because my father never talked about it, and it didn't occur to us to ask. We were kids and youngsters with our own lives to get on with. And would he have told us it if we had asked? Somehow I don't think so. Besides, how could he talk about it—things that had happened out there, in another reality. Trying to put it into words was impossible. Words are inadequate, a pale reflection of the real thing. Better not to mention anything at all than to suffer the frustration of trying to explain and then not being understood.

The Eternal Day

From here

He's always been here, way up north, the most hellish place on earth. This is it. This is his life. There is nothing else. Time standing still. The sun, always there, always low above the sea. Round and round, just above the horizon it goes, day and night. Never settles, never dips below, round and round. The sky aflame with fire, red, orange, copper, yellow and green. The perpetual light piercing his eyes. He never goes to bed, always scanning the sea around him, eyes glued to the binoculars, hurting, smarting, watering, redder than after an all-night party. No party. Only the ship chugging on and on. The convoy chugging on and on, 52 ships when they set out. God knows how many are left. Ships are all around him—port, starboard, ahead, astern . . . Straining his eyes scouring the surface for a torpedo trail or a periscope. Air vibrating with the sound of engines. Angels flying low above the ships, long white gowns trailing behind them, white wings glittering in the sun. The dead clambering on board, dripping water and seaweed, seeking the heat of the funnel. His grandmother among them wearing a red party dress, talking to him, looking much like when she was alive: 'Take it easy, my son, soon be over, soon be over,' disappearing into thin air, her voice lingering on 'soon be over'.

Air humming, the vibrating sound of the sun beating down on the sea. And mixed with the hum and the vibrations of the sun—the buzz of planes from the south. Like bees black against the burning sky. Coming closer. Always in waves, part of the day, part of the sun. No telling when they'll turn up, dropping bombs now, one narrowly missing his ship, exploding, sending a huge jet of water onto the deck, ship rocking but staying afloat. He nearly fell over. Another bomb hitting a ship further away, on port. Pouf! And into the air it went, a column of fire and it's gone. Another ship belching flames.

84

And suddenly, no idea why, the planes stop attacking and return whence they came, like birds disappearing into the distance. Silence. Only the hum of the engine and the drone of the universe, the vibration of the sun and the screams of men in the water. He covers his ears but the drone and vibration doesn't stop.

Telegram from the Commodore: "You're free." Code for renewed attack expected, convoy disperse.

Soon alone. Nothing but sea and the burning sky. Something floating on the water, tiny, drawing nearer, a lifeboat. One man waving, more men on board. Kristoffer sees it and gives the order: 'Survivors on starboard, change course for rescue'. Again he's the captain. Again he's in charge. The sun has gone quiet and the drone of the universe can no longer be heard.

To here .

USS Bunker Hill burning 1945 (Wikimedia commons)

Norway Early March 1944

The first sun of spring is pouring through the window. Outside a white film of frost is covering the trees, glittering, like diamonds. During the night a hard crust has formed on top of the deep and soft snow. From her window Martha can see that a layer of grey cloud is blowing in from the west. It's going to be a cold and blustery day which means that the snow crust will remain hard throughout the day so people can walk on it without leaving footprints. Outside her window a blue-tit is singing his short silvery tunes. He's been at it all morning, the most humble singer of all, yet the most welcome as he's the first bird to herald the coming of spring.

Oh no, there's that German soldier again, standing in the middle of the field looking straight at her window. So far she hasn't had much trouble from Germans, being dark-haired and brown-eyed she's of little interest to them. They prefer the Aryan type, seducing blonde girls with cigarettes and chocolates and nylon stockings. The silly airheads think the soldiers are in love with them; in love! They are the enemy. If a German soldier talks to you, you blank him, completely, continue walking or whatever you're doing, pretend he isn't there. Like last summer when she was walking home from the shops and she met a group of German soldiers where the road runs near the lake. Two of them started talking to her, pointing to the lake, asking her to come swimming, or worse. She continued walking, her heart pounding, nobody in sight, they could do anything. But then a third soldier said to them: "come". And they left her. She understood that, *come* being the same word in Norwegian. But there he is, staring towards her window. What gives him the right? But then they don't need to be given any right, do they; they just help themselves, like they've helped themselves to her country.

Anders is home. She heard his voice downstairs a minute ago. Anders and Marie on the ground floor, she and Bjørn on the first. A cosy little flat they have, sloping ceilings. She's got together some nice pieces of furniture. Kristoffer will be pleased with her when he gets home. If he gets home . . . So far he's alive, at least he was alive until a few weeks ago, as the parcels from Sweden keep coming she knows that he's out there, somewhere. Her sister, Johanna, married a Swede called Gustav Glad and lives in Stockholm. Kristoffer somehow sends money to Gustav and he and Johanna buy food stuff they can't get in Norway and send it on to her. No contact between the sailors and their families in occupied Norway, but they can send things via Sweden. Not everyone is lucky enough to have such a contact.

That German is still there. With the sun streaming through the window he can probably look straight into her room. She calls out: "Anders! Anders! Come up here." A door opens and she hears her brother's footsteps on the stairs. He has seen the German too, thinking what Martha is thinking. He puts his arms round her the way a husband would, after that they sit down at the table, pretending to talk normally. If things had been normal, they would have been having coffee, but no such luxury, you can get some sort of substitute but it tastes so foul you're better off with water. They make a point of not looking through the window, and when they finally do, the German is gone.

Anders says he was thinking to walk to the local shop, why doesn't she come with him, who knows, they might have got something in worth buying, the thing is to keep an eye out. Marie is coming too, doesn't want to be alone in the house with that Jerry on the prowl. Anders going shopping . . . it happens more and more often these days, but what is he really going for? Until a year ago he left all the shopping to Marie, and everybody knows there isn't much point in going to the little shop as there is hardly ever anything worth buying . . . brown flour mixed with sawdust, sometimes fish pudding that stinks of ammonia, some sort of grey margarine substitute. Or, perhaps a slither of real meat; or a small tin of corned beef from Argentina, it only happened once, but it did happen, so you can always hope. Martha and Marie understand what Anders' sudden shopping expedition on a bright Tuesday morning really means, but they don't say anything. Best not to know. Anders does what Anders must do. Marie doesn't like it, has nightmares about the Gestapo hammering on their door at night, ransacking the house and dragging Anders off for questioning, and everybody knows what that entails. Or worse, like what happened to the young resistance man who used to live in the old house between the road and the river on the way to Oslo. One night he was sitting at home with his mother. There was a knock on the door. Alarmed, mother and son went to open. Outside stood two SS officers. One of them said to the mother, nicely and politely: "Please could you step aside for a moment," and then he shot her son, point blank, dead on the spot, just like that, whereupon they said good bye and left.

Martha puts on her coat. It used to be so beautiful, bottle green, lovely pale-green silk lining. Kristoffer bought it for her in one of the best shops in Oslo back in 1938. But look at it now; the sleeves frazzled, the colour fading, the beautiful lining in shreds. If she'd had any inkling of what was in store she would have stocked up on clothes, bought material and wool to fashion clothing for herself and Bjørn, but who would have thought ... And no proper news since people had to turn in their radios to the Germans. They didn't want people to listen to London, to hear how the war was really going, "Deutschland siegt an alle Fronten"—Germany is victorious on all fronts. "Deutschland, Deutschland über alles"—Germany , Germany above all. How she hates that song! Anyway it isn't true. At least the Russians gave them one in the eye at Leningrad. News does filter through, slowly and patchily. Some brave people still have a radio hidden in the loft or under the hay in the barn and manage to listen to the Norwegian broadcasts from London.

* * *

Today the shop has a supply of knitting wool, bright green. Martha immediately thinks; jumper for Bjørn, but then she is only allowed two balls, two balls per child, that's the rule. Marie and Anders aren't entitled to any as they are childless. Martha buys the wool anyway. She can always find use for it. She can unpick one of her old sweaters and reuse the wool—the grey one with the worn-through elbows, and knit a grey jumper with green stripes. Should be enough for two small jumpers, one for little Ingrid as well, the youngest daughter of her brother Karl. She doesn't have much, poor thing. Her mother is sickly and coping badly with three children and food shortages. Martha helps them when she can. In the shop Anders points to a loaf of bread, horrible and grey and rock hard. Mrs Hagen, the shop keeper, takes the loaf saying she'll wrap it up in the back room. Two minutes later she emerges with it wrapped in an old newspaper, only the parcel seems too heavy to contain a loaf of bread. Anders places it in the bottom of his battered old rucksack with Martha's wool plus some coffee substitute that Marie had bought on top. A Jerry is stood in the doorway watching them. Act normal. Don't talk too much, sudden bursts of conversation have the opposite effect, making you look like you're talking in order to **look** normal, a real give-away if you've got something to hide. Forget about the parcel, if you forget, you'll look innocent, if you think of it, it will show in your body language and Jerry will get suspicious. More Germans outside. The hotel is full of them. At the beginning of the war they sent the owner packing and annexed the hotel. A few Norwegian women in threadbare clothing around the shops. Marie is itching to get away but stops to chat with them—as is her habit, Martha joins in. Act normal. Anders waits in the background, looking bored and impatient—women! Act normal! Martha goes to the post office.

There is a parcel from Gustav Glad. Martha signs for it and puts it in Anders' rucksack. The parcel looks battered, like it has been opened and wrapped up again. So the Germans have had their filthy hands on it, helping themselves to the best bits no doubt, or looked for contraband which they won't find. No matter. She opens the parcel on the kitchen table: A kilo of proper white flour! A yellow cheese with caraway seeds, Bjørn's favourite. A small bag of pure white sugar and a cured sausage. That's all. There must have been more, normally Gustav and Johanna slip in some cakes and a bar or two of chocolate for Bjørn, but nothing of the kind. Martha doesn't understand how Kristoffer does it; apparently you can send money and letters to neutral Sweden but not to occupied Norway. The cheese is wrapped in two layers of greaseproof paper, she undoes them, and there folded and tucked between the waxy crust and the cheese itself is a 100 kroner bill. Johanna and Gustav are crafty. Slipping in some goodies that the Germans can help themselves to. Having had their fill of sweetmeats and seeing no contraband they're too dim to search for anything else. Other times the cakes and chocolates do arrive, so there is no telling.

No letter from Kristoffer. She hasn't had a word from him since before the war. Weird, one would have thought that if he really wanted to he would have found a way to get a letter through, same as the money. Oh well; as long as the parcels keep coming they know he's alive and that he hasn't forgotten them completely. She knows that the tide of war has turned and that Germany is no longer victorious on all fronts. Perhaps it will soon be over. The soldiers on guard are getting younger by the day which must mean that the Germans are scraping the barrel. One such soldier used to hang around her parents' farm, God knows why, possibly to make sure they didn't sell any produce on the black market, or keep more than their quota. He looked cold and forlorn and not a day over 16. Her father felt sorry for him and gave him a piece of bread from time to time. He's gone now, perhaps to the Eastern Front to be slaughtered, who knows.

White flower and sugar. She still has a knob of the butter Kristoffer's mother sent them. Milk she gets every day from Anders' and Marie's cow. Two eggs and she's away, Bjørn will have pancakes for dinner. She cuts off a chunk of the cheese and goes downstairs to Marie, Anders had gone off into the forest, rucksack on his back and axe in hand to chop firewood. Good. That means that the parcel, whatever it contains, is no longer in the house. Marie is glad of the cheese and gives Martha two eggs in return. She even gives her a handful of blueberries that she's had preserved since summer so Martha can make blueberry jam for the pancakes.

Martha won't start making the pancakes until Bjørn is back from school. What if he brings that Nazi kid with him again? The boy, Arne, is nice enough, poor thing, but all the parents are weary of him. He and Bjørn are at school together, walk the two kilometres to and fro each day. They are the only boys of the same age who live around here. She can't tell Bjørn not to walk with him. But she has to be ever so careful of what she says in front of Bjørn lest he repeats it and Arne's parents get wind of it. You can't trust a traitor. Arne's father, Thorleif, might say something about her to the Germans to ingratiate himself with them. She was at school with him and his sister, Thora. She knows the family like she knows everyone else in this little place. Everybody knowing each other, keeping an eye out, knowing what their neighbour is up to. There has always been something different about Thorleif's family, thinking they were a cut above their neighbours, whatever gave them the idea. There are people like that; for no apparent reason they believe themselves to be better than ordinary folk, and now, with the Germans in charge, they see it as their chance to shine. Slimy creeps, running errands for their dirty masters. Thora is worse. Before the war she worked at the local hotel as a chambermaid cum waitress, as did Martha before she took herself off to Oslo to train as a chef, a profession she abandoned when she married. Thora sucked up to the owner of the hotel and before that she sucked up to their teacher. She is a year younger than Martha, Thorleif is a year older, but they were all in the same classroom. It was only a small country school with three year-groups being taught together. And now Thora is sucking up to the Nazis, once an arse-licker always an arse-licker. These days she's doing office work for the Germans, they must have taught her to lick stamps as well.

Anders never thought he was better than anyone, on the contrary. But look at him now! With his parcels and sorties for firewood into the forest where the boys of the resistance are hiding. All happening under Thorleif's very nose.

None of this is poor Arne's fault, and sometimes she'll share their food with him, as she can't stand the way he's eying their food when they're eating. Strangely his family seems to be as short of food as everyone else. But not the pancakes; that's too special, too much of a treat, besides he might talk about it at home and Thorleif might start wondering where she got the ingredients from. Has she perhaps got them on the black market . . . he could have her for that. No, Arne mustn't know about the pancakes.

There's Bjørn back from school now, and he's got Arne with him, two young boys coming up the path, best of friends as they should be, if only times had been normal. Up the stairs and into the kitchen they come. Arne two paces behind Bjørn. Both boys happy and excited: 'Mum, look, I got a chocolate!'

'Where did you get that from?'

'A German soldier gave it me. We were just walking and then he came and asked if we like chocolate.'

'And he gave me one too,' says Arne, 'look, and I haven't eaten it yet, I'll give half to Anton.'

'Arne, you know what,' Martha says, trying to sound friendly yet firm: 'I think you should take your chocolate and go home, now. Think how happy your brother will be.'

Arne's face looks disappointed and he lingers for a while, hoping for something to eat no doubt. Bjørn seems to understand that something is afoot and doesn't encourage him to stay. Reluctantly Arne puts on his mittens and leaves. Martha follows him with her eyes as he disappears down the path—looking lonely and forlorn.

Bjørn starts tearing open the chocolate wrapping.

'No, Bjørn, no, you mustn't eat it, come on, give it to me!'

'But why, mum, it's chocolate, the soldier gave it me.'

'Come on, you can't eat it.'

'But why?'

'Because it was given to you by a German, and decent Norwegians don't accept gifts from Germans!' The words nearly fell from her mouth but she bit her tongue in time and said:

'Because Hitler has weed on it. Don't you know, that's what he does, weeing on chocolates for his soldiers to give to children!'

'Oh,' Bjørn drops the chocolate and it lands on the floor.

Martha picks it up, carefully with two fingers, like she would a dead animal and chucks it into the wood-burning stove. 'And now, my good young man, I have a proper treat for you. Pancakes, real pancakes with blueberry jam. What do you say to that?'

Bjørn loved the pancakes; and a good thing too. He's grown quite a bit taller lately, but he's too skinny. His face looks gaunt and his ribs stick out. What would Kristoffer say if he saw him now? Bjørn had three pancakes and Martha had two, feeling guilty, but she couldn't stop herself. Hunger can make you do things you shouldn't. She had intended them all for Bjørn, but then she couldn't resist. At least there is enough batter left over for Bjørn to have two for breakfast in the morning.

Nearly dark outside, the long blue winter dusk that she loves. All the while she's been looking out of the window, hoping to see Anders emerging from the forest, and there he is, walking on the snow crust dragging a large bundle of firewood. Such a peaceable scene, like something out of the Middle Ages. The boys in the forest must have got their parcel, whatever it contains, dynamite perhaps. Anders makes straight for the woodshed. But what to do with all the firewood! There is simply too much of it. If the Germans or Thorleif come snooping and see it they might become suspicious. Tomorrow she'll tell Anders to give some of the wood to Karl, that's the best idea, and she will give them some of the white flour . . .

So far so good, but the night is long and the Gestapo might still come banging on the door.

1973–1943/44–2013

I have a soft spot for August bank holidays. They come as a surprise and I have never found out the reason for this long weekend at the tail end of summer when most people have recently been on vacation. Maybe it was intended for people who couldn't afford to go away, to offer them the chance of a day at the seaside before summer ran out . . . To me this bank holiday is tinged with nostalgia. It has to do with my very first bank holiday in England when we went on a daytrip to Brighton with the Egyptian students. We had only lived in London for two weeks and it was our first venture outside the city. The Egyptian students had hired a coach and we joined them on account of Maher being Egyptian and having enrolled for an MSc at Imperial College. Back home in Norway my father was still alive, and would be for another ten years.

It wasn't raining when we arrived in Brighton, but it was cold and blustery and difficult to determine whether the droplets in the air came from the sea or above. However, the pebble beach was full of people in deck chairs, wearing coats and covered in blankets—weirdest thing I'd seen in my life. I had heard about British eccentricities and this had to be one of them. We took a walk on the pier, a novel experience as there is nothing like it in Norway. I can't remember what we did for lunch, chips on the beach most likely. Definitely not a restaurant as our meagre resources had to be eked out till we found jobs to support ourselves.

We left Brighton as darkness started to fall, or perhaps it was the rain that made it look like dusk. What I remember best is sitting at the front of the coach, contemplating the green and melancholy landscape and wondering what on earth I had done to my life.

What has stuck in my mind ever since is the cheerless spectacle of people "sunbathing" in the blustering wind and drizzle. The gloomy weather matched my mood and feelings of having irrevocably messed up my life. I should have been in Oslo for the start of the new term at university, finishing

93

my degree in Spanish. I was taking one language degree course after the other in those days, mainly out of passion and interest but also because I envisaged a life of travelling the world as a multilingual interpreter.

40 years since that first bank holiday in Brighton, and at the time only 30 years since my father made entries in the diary that is now in front of me. A little black diary with his name written in pencil on the back of the front cover, slightly bent from sitting in his back pocket and taking the shape of his body, absorbing his sweat, and with it his DNA. John found three of Dad's wartime diaries in his trunk in the attic and he lent them to me on condition that I treat them with care and return them when I have finished with them.

My father's 1943 diary

The diaries explained something that had been a mystery to me. From my father's stories and anecdotes I'd had the impression that he was often in India during the war. I had also heard talk of a ship named Havprins (Ocean Prince). Yet the Herbrand records show that he must have spent 1941-1945 mainly criss-crossing the North Atlantic. The diaries for 1943 and 1944 clarified the mystery. My father spent 1943/44 on the Havprins, sailing mainly between India and the Persian Gulf, whilst the Herbrand continued negotiating the North Atlantic. Instead of chugging backwards and forwards across the icy Atlantic he was braving the monsoons and oppressive heat and humidity of the Indian Ocean.

To retrace my father's movements for the rest of the war, I shall put the Herbrand records aside and instead focus on his diaries. I know one thing for certain though. Dad always regarded the Herbrand and later on the Tank Empress as his special ships. From passing remarks I also know that he did come to Liverpool during the war. This indicates that the records of Herbrand's voyages until late 1942 in all likelihood do describe my father's whereabouts during those years.

Strategically the Indian Ocean was as important as the Atlantic, only less known to us as it all took place away from our shores. Britain and the USSR saw the newly opened Trans-Iranian Railway as an attractive route to transport supplies from the Persian Gulf to the Soviet region. This supply route became known as The Persian Corridor. The Allies delivered all manner of material to the Soviets, from Studbaker US6 trucks to American B-24 bombers, and oil of course. Most supplies in the corridor arrived by ship at Persian ports, and were then carried north by railway or in truck convoys. Some goods were reloaded onto ships to cross the Caspian Sea, others continued by truck. Axis naval forces gave a high priority to disrupting Allied Indian Ocean trade. Initial anti-shipping measures of unrestricted submarine warfare and raiding ships expanded to include airstrikes by aircraft carriers and raids by cruisers of the Imperial Japanese Navy. A Kriegsmarine Monsun Gruppe of U-boats operated from the eastern Indian Ocean to prevent essential supplies from reaching the Soviet Union.

As in the North Atlantic the worst threat was constituted by the German Submarines—on the prowl, lurking under water, plucking ships from the surface like a hunter plucking birds from the sky.

Dad never told us much about the Indian Ocean nor about his sojourns in India (what is now Pakistan). Sometimes he would talk of the dirt in the street, of camels pulling carts, of cows wandering down the street, of children flocking around him begging for baksheesh, of toothless old women reaching out their hands saying 'no father, no mother, no sister, no brother, baksheesh, Maharaja, baksheesh'. He spoke about the unbearable humid heat of the Gulf—of men who fainted with heat stroke and had to be put in the cool room. Sitting here, so many years later, I only remember two specific episodes: Once he went with a family who lived in India (British or Norwegian I don't know) to a restaurant to have curry. They had their ten year old daughter with them. The curry was extremely hot, and suddenly the little girl said: 'Look at my lips.' The skin was flaking. The curry had eaten it away. There is also the enormous white sapphire pendant with a matching ring that my father bought for my mother in India. A rich Indian lady had ordered the huge sapphire for a ring and then decided she didn't want it after all. My father had come across it, asked to have it made into a pendant and bought it, plus a matching ring. Both items are now in my possession. I don't find much use for the pendant, but I sometimes wear the ring.

When telling his anecdotes he seldom said exactly where or when an episode had taken place. This follows through to his diaries. The entries are dated due to the dates being already printed, but he tends not to indicate the location—quick notes, short and to the point, serving more as a record of his work than of his life. As there are often several blank pages between entries, it's impossible to work out the place from the context. The 1943 diary is particularly bad in this respect. All the same this diary tells the story of a frustrating year. A year of long stays in harbours because of engine trouble and lengthy repairs and waiting for spare parts to arrive, correspondence and telegrams backwards and forwards to Lloyds and the Nortraship offices. A year of much illness among the crew, one sailor passed away in hospital and was buried in the British cemetery, but no indication as to which country. There were incidents of sailors not turning up for work due to drunkenness, or going ashore without permission, of staying out all night and even getting in trouble with the local police. So, his life was not only about dodging submarines and defending the ship against German aeroplanes and warships, it was also about endless admin work, engine break downs and sick and unruly sailors. I'll include some of the relevant entries:

Friday January 1, 1943: *And may the New Year bring happiness to my people. Drive around Aden, visited the ancient dams.*

Thursday January 7: *Crew played football against the crew of Sophocles.*

At the beginning of February two men were taken to hospital, one of them with suspected appendicitis. The following day one of them was reported to be very ill, and one more man admitted to hospital. A new ordinary seaman came on board and, underlined, hit the sack! A week later one of the men is back from hospital and the Frist Engineer is under the influence and not working. On February 14 a Mr Hansen is in trouble for unauthorised shore leave and staying out all night . . . And so it goes on. Nothing as to where this all took place in Bombay, Karachi or Aden?

Friday March 26: *Bought pig on board the b/s* (I think it says) *Nicaragua, Rs 325.* I think this is referring to Yemeni Rias, which means that he must have been in the Yemen at the time.

Monday April 12: *Hansen, Hole and Aronsen drunk and not working.*

April 13: *Hansen, Hole and Aronsen not working or barely working due to drunkenness.*

April 14: *Hansen and Aronsen called in and informed that their conduct will be logged.*

April 15: *Hansen not working. Has suffered a minor stroke. Aronsen, Dahle, Brekke sent ashore to see doctor.*

Monday May 17: *Flag hoisted. Feast on board. Later visit to Mrs and Mr Eng.* May 17 is Norway's constitution day. The Germans had forbidden all celebration of May 17 in Norway as well as any display of the Norwegian national flag. But here, somewhere by the Indian Ocean the day was duly celebrated.

Saturday May 29: *Jørgensen and W. Capes to see doctor. K. A. Mathiessen taken to hospital with leg injury. His clothes and information about payment sent ashore by motorboat. Left Aden at 21.20.*

After this only a few entries about admin and various engine troubles, waiting for spare parts and spare parts finally arriving. On June 17 he flies from Karachi to Bombay where he visits the Nortraship office and is told that the necessary repairs will be performed in Karachi.

Saturday June 26: *Visited the Norwegian Vice Consul. The rudest individual I have ever encountered. He declared that I was of no interest to him.*

More entries about crew members in or out of hospital. Trouble with engine-shaft and pistons.

Wednesday August 4: *Casualty list to Lloyds.* That's all, no details about the casualties or how they occurred.

Monday August 23: Scribbled in the margin next to a long entry about arriving in Abadan: *Temperature in the shade, 45 degrees.*

Saturday September 4: *In convoy across the Indian Ocean. 03.50, engine stops due to broken piston. Piston replaced. Lost the convoy. Full speed ahead.*

September 5: *Trying to catch up with the convoy.*

September 6: *Indian Ocean, uneventful day. Engine works well. Arrived Bombay harbour 15.18.*

Tuesday October 12: *Received U-boat warning and all cannons fully manned.*

Sunday November 14: *Second Engineer resigned because of quarrel with First Engineer. Both of them drunk.*

November 15: *Second Engineer not working.*

November 16: *Second Engineer back to work.*

After what looks like a frustrating year we finally reach December 31: *The year has come to an end. Like last year we are in harbour with engine trouble. The atmosphere is somewhat down-cast because of this long stay in the harbour, but we hope to be off before too long. The end of the year is marked with good wishes for the New Year. We'll see what it will bring. We expect to get back home.*

And then it's 1944. Another little pocket diary, pale green this time, the back coming undone. "Diary 1944" written in fancy copper coloured letters on the cover. Inside the cover; a tiny black and white drawing of the Taj Mahal. The diary was printed in Karachi which is where he has been stuck for some time due to engine trouble.

His first entry in the little green diary of 1944 reads: *Sunday January 2nd 1944. Diamantis back from hospital. Party on board the "Thorshavn". After that cinema to see "Edge of Darkness".* From a later entry it transpires that he celebrated New Year in Karachi. How long he had been there we don't know.

Tuesday January 4: *Informed that the repairs of the connecting bolts in Calcutta have not yet started.*

Wednesday January 5: *Dinner on board the "Høgh Silver Scout" with Consul Gylseth and wife. After that conference with various authorities re. supplies.* Not the rude Vice Consul who wanted nothing to do with him.

No further entries until May 4 when he writes: *Pilot on board 14.30. Left Karachi 15.30.*

On May 10 he arrives in Shat Al Arab at 03.45.

The notes are sparse. Nothing of interest until Sunday June 4 when he writes: *Repair was completed at 13.30. Went ashore for sailing route. Sailed from Bombay at 19.00. One gunner and two able seamen left behind.*

The men must have been messing about in Bombay and not made it back to the ship in time. The sailing route must be what was often referred to as "the Envelope" with instructions of destination, where to assemble for the convoy and the route. The Envelope was sealed and not to be opened until the ship was at sea. There were plenty of German spies about and if the Envelope fell into the wrong hands the Germans would know where exactly to find the convoy. Without this knowledge they would have to waste time searching for it, even if they usually located it in the end.

Tuesday June 6. Big letters written in ink, he normally used a pencil. *Invasion of Europe started this morning.* He was referring to D-day.

June 10: *No wind and the air is slightly misty.*

Saturday July 1: *Able seaman Frøysland who lately has been drinking heavily was today in some kind of delirium, fantasising about the mirror, sounds etc. We sent for an ambulance and he was taken to Bombay hospital.*

July 15: *Frøysland signed off.*

Thursday July 20: *22.10, reported to Khor Khuwair.*

Thursday July 27: *Hopelessly oppressive heat. Atmosphere extremely close and humid.*

August 14, one entry written in red ink. It simply says: *Invasion of Southern France.*

Short entries about the weather: Extremely hot and oppressive. Sometimes a fresh breeze, sometimes rain. Detailed descriptions of the monsoon winds. Very hot and humid. One entry says dangerous wind. Temperature falls below 30.

Thursday August 17: *Temperature ca. 34. Weather is good. Unusual for these waters.*

August 24: *Temperature at 06.00, 26 degrees, it feels quite cool.* Then on August 28: *Strong monsoon from south-west. Wind drops towards evening.*

August 31: *11.30, arrived in Aden. 14.40 went ashore by motorboat to take the chief steward to see a doctor for examination of swelling in his seat. New supplies on board. 19.30, left Aden.*

Nothing of much interest until September 8 when he writes: *05.30, Boarding Officer on board. 06.30, anchored at Suez Bay.*

Monday September 11: *Sailed through the Canal. Arrived Port Said at 19.40.*

He left Port Said at 13.40 on September 12.

On Friday September 14 he writes: *Changed station from 54 to 62,* meaning that he is part of a large convoy.

On September 15 he receives orders from the Commodore that his destination is Augusta, southern Sicily.

On Saturday 16 he had to leave the convoy on account of steering problems. The steering was fixed and he caught up with the convoy at 06.00 on the 17th. He only stayed with the convoy till 14.30 when he broke off and sailed to Augusta.

The following weeks are spent sailing between various Mediterranean ports until he leaves Gibraltar on October 12.

Then nothing until October 23 when he writes: *10.00, received order from the Vice Commodore: "Your destination is New York."*

November 16, New York: *Left Havprins. Did not sign off.* And then, the following day: *Signed off from Havprins.*

The years of stress and frustration have taken their toll. On the 20th of November he visits a Dr Emery and a Dr Duckworth who takes X-rays. He starts treatment for sinusitis with Dr Emery on the 22nd. He also suffers from eczema on his chest which is treated by a Dr Kerr who takes a blood sample. Then nothing until December 10th when Dr Kerr finishes the treatment and he gets the result of his blood test which is 100% OK.

On December 11 he receives news from Nortraship that Herbrand is undergoing repairs in England and will remain there for several months. This indicates that the Herbrand is still seen as HIS ship.

The next entry is on December 24th, Christmas Eve, very important for Norwegians, as that's when we have our main celebration. He simply writes: *Dinner with Watts.*

December 25: *Dinner at Saron Appleseth's with Mathias Fure and Mathias Renstad.* Mathias Fure was a relative from back home who had made his life in New York.

On December 26th, Dr Emery informs him that his left sinus is as good as healed.

Sunday December 31: *Ross. Pleasant evening with Watts at Prince George Hotel. Festive dinner in "the Old English Tea Room" during which the old year bowed out.*

And so passed another year of my father's life. The entries in his diary are short and irregular, and he does not give many details, this was perhaps out of necessity, the pages are tiny. But would he have added more detail if he'd had more space . . . like the sights and sounds of Bombay or Aden? Probably not. He was a man of action rather than a writer. A man of the moment, who lived through his job, took each day as it came and was little given to reflection and contemplation.

We think that the past is dead and gone. But that is not so. Some little bit will always remain. I'm contemplating his three diaries; there is one for 1945 as well. These were his diaries. The 1944 one bought in India, the 1945-one in New York, the 1943-one I don't know where . . . All three of them carried with him backwards and forwards across the oceans. When the temperature hit the 30s, they felt the heat. When the air was damp and rainy, they absorbed the humidity. After the war they went with him to Norway where they came to rest in the attic where John found them and lent them to me. And here they are on my desk in London, next to my laptop, an invention never dreamed of when Dad sailed the Indian Ocean and wrote brief notices about weather, departures, engine trouble and destinations plus the odd sentence about things that intrigued him. The handwriting is compressed and sometimes illegible, most of it in pencil, but surprisingly fresh-looking.

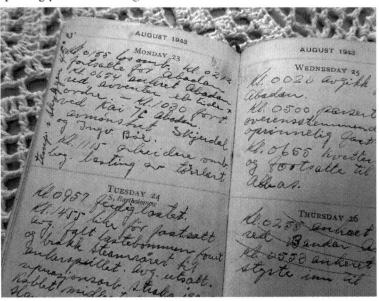

Some of the longer entries in one of my father's diaries

All the things I paid no attention to when he was there and I could have asked him. . . . What he did tell us more often than not went in one ear and out the other. He sailed a lot on the Persian Gulf and because it was called the Persian Gulf I assumed it to be Persia, but it could have been any of the oil rich Gulf States. Besides, John and I were only young, living in the safety of post-war Norway with our own lives to get on with. Dad was away at sea and that was it. Letters arrived with large exotic stamps, much more interesting than the tiny Norwegian stamps with an image of the King or the Norwegian Lion, our national symbol. We too wrote letters and sent them to his Head Office in Oslo; from there they were forwarded to wherever his ship, the Tank Express, would next be arriving. Dad often spoke about Aden in the Yemen, but without making it clear that he had been there a lot during the war. Here is something I do remember him telling us, but that happened in the 1950s: He was flying from Aden on the first leg of his homeward journey. As the plane took off long flames shot out from one of the engines. The pilot stopped the plane, the passengers were evacuated and nobody was hurt. However, they had to remain in Aden for a few days until the engine had been repaired and were accommodated in a, for Aden, luxury hotel. One day Dad saw two Yemini men dragging a dead animal, head, fur and all, towards the kitchen entrance of the hotel. The sight so revolted him that he lived on bred and fruit for the rest of his stay there. He spoke about the unbearable heat and humidity of the Gulf; that they had to take salt tablets to compensate for the body's loss of salt through perspiration. Once the sweat had been pouring from him to such a degree that two puddles had formed on the floor. Strangely, my father, the ginger-haired and pale skinned "Viking", seemed to cope better with the heat than darker people from warmer climes.

But what about me and Brighton? After 16 years in North London we moved to a suburb on the edge of South London where we now live. From here it's only an hour's drive to Brighton and we have made the journey innumerable times, first with the boys and later on Maher and I on our own.

Some things have changed. Never again have I seen people "sunbathing" in the wind and rain decked out in coats and blankets. Gone is the notion that a day at the seaside is a precious day whatever the weather and has to be spent on the beach.

One thing that never changes is the sea. I don't like to be on it, but I can contemplate it for hours—to simply gaze at the immense expanse of water . . . the way it reflects the colours of the sky, the gold and silver of the sunshine. Seagulls shrieking. Ships sailing by, some looking like my father's Tank Empress, which I remember clearly. The surf breaking against the shore, the tide washing in and out . . .

1945

A new year and a new diary, again a little black one, bought at Commercial Stationary Co., 15 Whitehall St., New York. There is a stationer's stamp on the first page.

My father spends all of January in New York, perhaps the nearest thing to a holiday in years. Not all holiday, though. On January 9 he writes: *Finished treatment with Dr Emery. In all 24 treatments, still not well.* Nothing as to what sort of treatment. He attends several work related meetings. Also he appears to have been grappling with bureaucracy, e.g. a dispute with Nortraship regarding his salary for the Havprins period and with Norwegian National Insurance to have his medical expenses refunded. The disputes seem to have had a satisfactory outcome as he makes notes of the money he's been receiving. On January 6th there was a party for him at St George Hotel, Brooklyn: *And a good time was had by all.* Most likely the party was in aid of his birthday, he was born on the 6th of January 1902, and so was 43 years old.

I'm trying to picture the world that my father encountered in New York during the winter of 1944-45, a haven after the dangers of the open seas, the bombed-out cities of Britain and the disease-ridden Indian and Gulf cities. But New York, back to civilisation as we know it—well-dressed and healthy looking individuals, so different from the threadbare and emaciated people of Liverpool. Apparently the St George Hotel is still there. What was it like back then? There must have been ladies in fashionable clothes, neat perms and bright lipstick, a little hat glued to their heads. And music! A band or a pianist, playing Glenn Miller who had lost his life on December 15th when his plane disappeared over the English Channel. Or perhaps they were playing Cole Porter who was at the height of his fame with songs like *Night and Day* and *I get a kick out of you.* Or the songs of bright young stars like Frank Sinatra and Bing Crosby. I love the music of the 1940s—some of the first songs I listened to as a child. They transport me to a time I can only glimpse from films and my father's memories. And you still hear them—on the radio or in shops and restaurants. And, courtesy of technology you can listen to them on YouTube whenever you like.

Throughout January the name Ross keeps cropping up. *Out with Ross . . . spent the evening at Ross' . . . nice evening with Ross etc.* Who was she? I like to believe that she was a woman he had met in one of the parties he attended. Captains of Norwegian ships were often invited into sophisticated circles. Norwegian sailors were popular on account of Norway giving Hitler a run for his money: "Small nation standing up to the Germans", and people knew that the Norwegian commercial fleet was invaluable to the war effort. My father had a weakness for beautiful and sophisticated women. I have no idea who Ross might have been. Warm, beautiful, elegant, dark hair, red lipstick, she must have had dark hair. Norway is full of blonde women so popular elsewhere, but the epithet "Scandinavian blonde" would never be used by anyone from Scandinavia. In Norway dark hair and brown eyes were seen as exotic and therefore attractive. Who can blame him for finding a love interest? Year in, year out at sea, away from home. His wife loosing substance like a fading photograph. But Ross, lively, warm, sophisticated . . . or so I imagine. Her husband an officer fighting somewhere abroad may-be. I'll never know.

On January 22nd he is trying to clarify a rumour that Herbrand will be undergoing repairs for quite some time. The Herbrand is clearly seen as his ship, and there seem to be plans afoot for Kristoffer to resume command of her. Apparently she had been involved in a collision which would explain why she needed extensive repairs.

On January 25 he writes: *Informed that Herbrand is in Greenock, Scotland, and that the repairs are expected to be completed towards the end of March. Will be taking G.C. Brøvig to England around 2 February.*

January 29: *Told to take over G.C. Brøvig for crossing to England. Visited the ship. Pleasant evening with Ross.*

January 30. *Brought my clothes on board the G.C. Brøvig. Out with Ross.*

February 1: *Took command of the G.C. Brøvig. Boarded at 10.20.* (This would be am as he operates with the 24 hour clock.)

February 7: *Left New York harbour 02.55.*

Thursday February 8: *Strong easterly breeze, heavy rain showers. Warmer and better weather towards evening. Ship rolling.*

February 9: *Strong westerly breeze. Rain showers.*

Saturday 10: *Strong north-westerly breeze. Rough seas. 01.20 a life boat amidships was lifted off its hook and lost. Met Halifax convoy.*

February 12, Monday: *Fog during first part of the day. Speed around 9 knots. Lots of depth charges.*

February 13: *Good weather. Some snow. Speed around 10.2 knots. Snowstorm towards evening.*

February 14: *Fresh westerly wind with snow showers.*

And so the G.C Brøvig slowly chugs her way across the Atlantic. Unfamiliar ship, unfamiliar crew, although Kristoffer is probably too long in the game to be unnerved by the situation. But the depth charges—mainly fired from the escorting corvettes . . . a sure sign that there are U-boats on the prowl and attacking. With the snowstorm, impossible to spot the torpedo trail. Besides, the hours of darkness are longer than the hours of light. He hasn't got his gramophone any more. Perhaps it's still on the Herbrand, time will tell. February 15th and 17th. Entries about the weather like the strength of the wind, waves and precipitation.

Sunday 18: *Weather improved. Fuelled corvette. Started at 10.00 and finished at 13.15.* This means that the G.C. Brøvig was acting as escort oiler.

February 19: *Wind from south-west. Emergency turn to avoid U-boat. The Americans made soup. Changed position from 13 to 52 in the convoy. New U-boat warning in the evening. Broke off from the main convoy.*

Two points here: In Norwegian "make soup" can be a euphemism for making trouble. It could therefore mean that American crew members had somehow been disruptive. Or; in English you **cook** food, whereas in Norwegian you **make** food. Bar the odd English word or expression my father wrote in Norwegian. Consequently it could simply mean that the Americans had cooked a pot of soup to brighten a gruelling crossing. The second interesting point: According to one of my father's contemporaries (now deceased) his longevity in the convoys was partly due to him sometimes opting to break away. He believed it to be safer on his own whilst the U-boats were homing in on the convoy. However, until now this has basically been unsubstantiated hearsay. It's only now, upon reading my father's diary that I have the proof that there were indeed times when he decided to go it alone.

* * *

February 20: *Sunshine and good weather. One ship torpedoed at 12.55. Loads of depth charges.*

February 21, Wednesday: *Depth charges in the Irish Sea. 15.45 Pilot on board. 17.00 anchored in Greenock.*

Thursday 22: *Signed off from G.C. Brøvig. Staying at the Hotel Adelphi. Attended meeting with other captains. Letter from my wife.*

This is interesting because it says something about the logistics of the convoy system. If there was mail waiting for him in Greenock it can only mean that the whereabouts of each sailor must have been known to the Nortraship offices at all times. How else could a letter from my mother have been waiting for him in Greenock, and via which channels had she managed to send it? Another thought-provoking and rather sad point: The wording "letter from my wife", not Martha. Doesn't this indicate that after all this time, and going out with Ross, my mother must have seemed like a distant, almost irrelevant memory and a source of guilty feelings?

Greenock, February 22nd 1945

Difficult to understand what people are saying but he knew that already. Liverpool is just as bad. The taxi driver who drove him to his hotel kept chatting, meaning to be friendly no doubt. Nice man, not his fault that he had grown up with an impossible accent. Kristoffer did not wish to offend the man by constantly asking him to repeat so he interjected *yes* and *hm* and *that so*, in what he hoped were reasonably correct places. Anyway the man was busy driving. It was raining hard and the windscreen wipers could barely cope.

The receptionist at the Adelphi Hotel spoke clearly enough, a short and skinny young man with a slight limp and thinning black hair combed back from his face and held in place with pomade. The bad leg explained why he wasn't in the army or perhaps he had been, and been invalided out because of an injury. His navy suit was worn and shiny with use and the cuffs protruding from under the sleeves were frayed. UK of course, shortages of every kind, people looking down-at-heal and threadbare. The young man scrutinized his passport and his expression changed from sullen disinterest to affability and eagerness to please. Norwegians were popular wherever they went; the little nation that stood up to Hitler and kept fighting even when the battle was lost.

'Only the one night, Sir?'

'Yes, I'm taking over my ship tomorrow.'

He liked staying in hotels, especially on his own without any of his officers who invariably wanted to have drinks with him and to check out the neighbourhood bars, going on about people back home or problems with their crew or whatever. Too much. He wanted peace.

It had been a gruelling crossing. First the rough sea and the snowstorms, then the subs. He had broken off from the convoy in the end, safer that way, to sneak off on his own leaving the wolves to focus on the convoy. Not everyone could do it, you needed to have a feel for where the subs were lurking and grab your moment. He hadn't been to bed for two nights, and then only for a couple of hours of restless sleep. His legs aching with varicose veins hard and tender to the touch, an old person's complaint. He was only 43 and a man of 43 was not supposed to have varicose veins. His father was 65 the last time he saw him and his legs were smooth like a 20-year-old's. But he hadn't been standing on them for seventy hours in a row. Once he'd settled in on the Herbrand he would find a doctor to see what could be done. One of his molars was aching as well. A large filling fell out on his last day in New York and he'd had no time to go to the dentist. He had managed to will away the pain while at sea but now it attacked him with a vengeance. 43 years old, tired-out and in pain. Sometimes he regretted turning down the ship-supplier, Laszinsky's, offer to go into business with him and set up home in Trinidad. He couldn't see Martha agreeing to live in Trinidad. Much too different and she had never attempted to learn English. Other wives had at least taught themselves to string together a few sentences, or they'd been through secondary school and learnt English that way. Sometimes he had fantasised about setting up house with Ross in Trinidad. Now that would suit her—sun-tanned, elegant, entertaining clients—she'd be excellent at that. He would keep sending money to Martha of course, and Bjørn could attend boarding school in England, become an English gent. He had been fantasising along these lines, knowing full well that nothing would ever come of it. Ross' husband would be back from wherever he was stationed and Ross would never leave him. That's the nature of women, swearing undying love and at the same time being terrified that their husbands would find out. He'd said good bye to her in New York knowing that chances were he'd never see her again. He had drifted into New York on the tide of war and now the tide had carried him back out. A captain went where he was told to go, a glorified errand-boy; that was the reality of it. The two of them together in Trinidad . . . It could have worked but neither of them had had the courage to try.

In the office, when signing off from the G.C. Brøvik, there was a letter from Martha in between the communications from Nortraship. He'd recognised the large clever-schoolgirl handwriting right away. The envelope looked battered and worn; God knows how many by-ways it had travelled before finally reaching an office in Greenock. He felt it in his inside pocket. He would open it and read it tonight after a couple of whiskies.

Later, on his way to the dining room, he asked the receptionist if he knew about a good dentist. The damaged tooth would not stop bothering him. It was as if it was saying: 'Look, I pretty much left you in peace during the crossing and now it's my turn.' It wasn't too bad right now. In his room he had crushed an aspirin, mixed it with a drop of water and pasted it around the bad tooth. It numbed the pain almost right away, but only temporarily of course. It had started aching during the Captains' meeting. Not surprisingly.

Kristoffer hated meetings, always the people with the least to say making the most noise. Like that over-inflated Captain Bredesen, a man in his mid-forties who had spent most of the war years transporting sugar between the Caribbean islands and Texas. Finally he'd done an Atlantic crossing and at the meeting, in the company of some real heavy-weights, he'd been talking like an expert, like he knew it all when in fact he knew very little. He also appeared to be an expert on history and military strategy. Like most people who are all talk and no action he showed no awareness of the men around him shrugging, smirking and looking at their watches. In the end Kristoffer could stand it no longer and asked him: 'And how many Murmansk runs did you say you have done?' That had shut him up.

However, this meeting had had a lighter atmosphere than other such meetings Kristoffer had attended over the years. There was an air of optimism in the room that not even the rain lashing against the windows and Bredesen's inane chatter was able to dispel. Hitler was on his last legs, no doubt about it. Germany and Japan were being beaten on many fronts. The British and the Americans had bombed Dresden to smithereens. The bombing of Berlin and other German cities continued. Ecuador, Paraguay, Venezuela, Peru and Turkey had declared war on Germany and Japan. American naval vessels were bombarding Tokyo and Yokohama. Roosevelt, Churchill and Stalin had met in Yalta to discuss the post-war reorganisation of Europe.

The captains had left the meeting in a celebratory mood. Kristoffer had come across many of them over the years, and now they asked him to come for a drink with them. Normally he would have been happy to join them, but the damned tooth had been aching like mad; so he'd said no thank you, let's make it another day.

The receptionist wrote down a dentist's name and address on a piece of paper. He said he didn't really know anything about him as he hadn't seen a dentist for years, too expensive, but this one he knew had a nice big surgery so chances were that he was good. Outside the down-pour had not abated.

'Does it always rain here?' Kristoffer asked putting away the piece of paper.

'Aye, pretty much,' said an older man in a cap and a worn tweed jacket standing by the reception desk. A sheep farmer from out of town, Kristoffer thought, a breath from an older and safer world—a world that still existed here and there but which Kristoffer hadn't seen in years 'I don't suppose you know Ardmore?' the man continued.

Kristoffer couldn't say that he did. 'Ardmore is the small town opposite Greenock. When you can't see Ardmore it means that it's raining. If you can see it, it means that it's about to start.'

'I understand,' Kristoffer said, 'you mean if it isn't raining in Greenock it soon will be.'

Anyway, the weather didn't bother him. He thanked the receptionist for the address and made for the dining room.

There wasn't much of a menu. In the end he settled for leek and potato soup and something called Welsh rarebit with chips. The soup was thin and watery and the Welsh rarebit, a mixture of diced onions, cheese and eggs, the waiter had explained, was more onion than cheese and egg and the chips tasted of stale lard. Shortages of course. It was what people in Europe had had to put up with for years.

The dining room was friendly and warm. A blazing fire in the grate. The beer was good too, not as cold as he would have liked it, but good. There weren't many people in the room. For a moment Kristoffer was almost hoping that the sheep farmer would enter and want to join him seeing that they had become sort of acquainted, and perhaps invite him to his farm one day. He kept watching the door but the man never turned up. Just as well—a conversation with a stranger wasn't exactly what he needed. Two elderly ladies, probably locals, with grey permed hair kept in place with hairnets were sitting at the next table. One of them had a mangy-looking silver fox draped round her neck, its tiny head with its beady glass eyes dangling off one shoulder. Kristoffer hated the sight of dead animals. Having grown up on a farm where animals were routinely slaughtered he'd soon realised that he was not cut out to be a farmer. But the sea . . . How many times had he stood on the shore, watching the large ships as they sailed by, thinking; I'll have one like that one day. A long time ago now. Three burly young men in military uniforms, sipping pints of beer and talking loudly were standing by the bar. Kristoffer couldn't understand a word they were saying. A well-to-do couple sitting close by, eating Welsh rarebit as well. For one heart-stopping moment he thought he was looking at Ross, same dark hair in a bun at the nape of her neck, but of course it wasn't her. This lady was older, pale and discontented looking, not like Ross at all. But for a moment . . .

He ordered a large whisky to wash away the taste of lard and onion. His tooth had started aching again and in his inside pocket Martha's letter remained unopened.

1945. Peace at last

He boarded the Herbrand on February 23rd at the Great Harbour, Greenock, and signed on the very same day. From then on he is living on board his ship in his old quarters. He must have found his wind-up gramophone and his records because he brought them to Norway after the war. I remember them well: *La Cumparsita* . . . I thought it was spelt *La Comparasita,* but how could I know, I hadn't seen it written down since I read it on the record sleeve at the age of ten or so. Just now I found an ancient recording of it on YouTube, probably done during the war. Old and scratchy, a vanishing remnant of another time. Then there was Deanna Durbin singing Schubert's *Ave Maria*, which I also found on YouTube plus *The Vilja Song* from *The Merry Widow,* one of Mum's favourites—and more.

On March 2nd he sends money to Gustav Glad in Sweden, no doubt intended for my mother and Bjørn.

Whilst in Greenock he takes the opportunity to sort out some of his health issues. He mentions three visits to a dentist, the first one for extraction (obviously the bad tooth was beyond repair) and the last one for cleaning. He also visits a doctor for injections in his varicose veins, four in all.

Then there is the more-than-his job's-worth officer from Customs and Excise who sinks his teeth in and refuses to let go. He first visits the Herbrand on April 4th announcing that no declarable goods must be consumed. On the 5th he returns saying that no beer must be consumed without permission from the Captain. He turns up again the following day saying that they can drink the beer. Quote: "It's going and we forget about it." On the 10th he crops up maintaining, again, that no declarable goods must be consumed. The following day he's back reiterating that no declarable goods must be consumed. He claims that three gallons of spirits, a box of snuff and some cigars have gone missing. On the 13th he turns up for the umpteenth time asserting that they can use the beer but nothing else. On the 14th he's there again confirming that they can drink all the beer. The following days there is no sign of him and my father assumes that he has found somebody else to pester. But then, on the 20th, there he is harping on about the beer that he has already given them permission to drink. He turns up once more on the 24th, but that appears to be it. No further mention of him after that. But what made him harass my father in such a way—determined not to let him and his men get away with the tiniest drop of whisky or pinch of snuff. There are people like that, blinkered individuals who slavishly follow every rule or regulation no matter how pointless. I have never understood them. Or, perhaps it was simply the little man's jealousy towards a taller, stronger, more handsome and successful individual . . . A sad man of 40, living with his mother on one of the council estates on the outskirts of town, fixated on getting the better of this captain with his heroic and glamorous existence.

On March 23rd my father had a meeting with Consul Utne about decorations for certain crew members. The consul comes on board on the 27th and decorates four men.

I can't help thinking: What about Kristoffer Martin Elias Hoddevik, didn't he deserve a medal as well? How come nobody suggested a decoration for him! This lack of appreciation was to become a sore spot and source of much bitterness, but more about that later.

Towards the end of March and throughout April there are regular entries but mainly about technical and administrative matters. He is still in Greenock.

On April 4th he takes the train to Nottingham and continues to London Kings Cross where he checks in at the County Hotel. He has one or two meetings, one of them seems to have been about the future plans for the Herbrand; it's not quite clear from the diary. On the 7th he boards the train back to Glasgow. I don't know if this was when he saw Marble Arch. When he visited me in London many years later, he took the bus from North Finchley, where we lived, to Central London because he wanted to revisit Marble Arch. He said he had seen it during the war and wanted to see it again.

Back in Greenock there are more entries about administrative matters, crew members being signed off, new crew members signed on etc. Until, on April 30th in between other ordinary entries he has written in large red capitals: HITLER KILLED. At the time there was confusion about Hitler's death; German propaganda claimed he had died a hero's death fighting in Berlin, when in fact he had shot himself.

Then follow his longest entry ever:

Monday May 7: *13.00, report over BBC that the Germans in Norway appear to be withdrawing towards the Swedish border. 14.00, the BBC announces that Churchill will shortly be broadcasting that the war in Europe has come to an end. 15.00, the German Foreign Minister broadcasts from Hamburg that the war is over. 16.15, visit from British commander with greetings from Admiral Landers.*

May 8: *00.20, woken up from the sound of sirens and fireworks going off, mainly from British naval vessels. Peace is officially declared at 00.00 hours.* (Written in red): *15.00, speech by Churchill. Speech by the Crown Prince* (presumably the Norwegian Crown Prince Olav). And then: *16.30 . . .* (illegible handwriting) *. . . .commission landing in Oslo.*

May 9: *09.00, Norwegian Broadcasting Corporation opens with "God Bless our Precious Fatherland". Followed by speech by the chief of the Broadcasting Corporation, Olaf Midtun. NORWAY IS FREE.*

Listening to *God Bless our Precious Fatherland,* our National Hymn, must have been a moving experience. It was the first time he had heard it played on Norwegian radio since before the war, as the Germans had banned our National Anthem and all other music that could be seen as specifically Norwegian. Throughout the world Norwegian expats and refugees must have been glued to the radio for this broadcast. Fewer people inside Norway would have heard it. The Germans had forced people to hand in their radios to stop them from listening to the BBC and learning that the Germans were not as victorious on all fronts as they would have people in the occupied countries believe. A few brave individuals had managed to hang on to their radios—under the floorboards in the attic, under the hay in the barn and so on. Being caught with a radio usually meant prison camp. But now the radios were brought out into the open and family and neighbours sat clustered around them listening to this much-loved hymn for the first time in years:

> *God bless our precious Fatherland*
> *And make it bloom like a garden.*
> *Make your peace shine from mountain to shore*
> *And make winter flee from the sun of spring.*

Let people live together like brothers,
Like Christians are meant to do.

People crowding out into the streets in their worn-out and threadbare clothes, Norwegian flags in hand, strings of Norwegian flags around their necks. Larger size flags that had been gathering dust for five years were brought out and hoisted on every flagpole. People singing the national anthem: *Yes, We Love This Country.*

It was during these euphoric days that women who'd had German boyfriends or borne them children were dragged into the street and had their hair shorn off, unceremoniously and mercilessly, and their older children, who'd had nothing to do with it, shunned and banned from the celebrations. In the years to come many of the children born to German fathers, the so-called *Lebensborn,* were rejected and excluded to the point that any chance of a happy and fulfilling life was ruined. A dark chapter in Norwegian history.

* * *

There are no more entries in my father's diary until May 22 and 23 when he visits a doctor for injections in his right leg. He visits the doctor again on May 25.

On May 28 the repairs to the Herbrand are nearing completion.

Saturday June 2: *05.45, left Great Harbour for a test run. 14.00, anchored in Greenock Harbour. One piston overheated on port side engine.*

June 3: *Repair of port engine.*

June 4: *16.15, repairs completed and left Greenock.*

Thursday June 7: *The King returns to Oslo. Sent a telegram to Nortraship, Greenock, my first private telegram in 5 years.*

On Sunday July 1st the Herbrand is finally ready for its first North Atlantic Crossing in a long time. My father writes*: 05.20, finished loading. 07.25, papers on board. 07.30, pilot on board. 08.05, anchor away. 08.10, pilot left ship. 7 men left behind. 08.30 none of the men to be seen, so decided to sail without them.*

His first peace-time crossing since before the war.

We are in fact only talking about four years as he spent the first year after Norway was dragged into the war in relative safety around Central and South America. Four years is not long in an average lifespan. For many of us they slip away peacefully with little to distinguish one year from the next, at least when you reach a certain age: Holidays, your child graduating or getting married are islands in a sea of calm. Looking back, five or ten years seem like one or two and you can't understand what happened to the time. Not so when you are in an extreme situation. For my father the years at sea during the war must have felt like a lifetime and nobody who lived through them got out unscathed.

One tangible effect of his experiences was that he did not suffer fools and people with inflated opinions of themselves. He could not stand them, wanted nothing to do with them, and in his mind there were a great many such people about. Self-satisfied and pompous individuals who bragged and boasted of their mediocre achievements. Like some of the Norwegian resistance people. Many of them had demonstrated extreme courage and sacrifice and been tortured to death or perished in German concentration camps. Or, returned from the camps with lasting physical or psychological damage, like two of my teachers at secondary school. One had been so undernourished that he had lost the ability to put on weight and looked like a skeleton. Another looked like a man of 70+ but was in fact 47 years old. One of our neighbours was a hopeless alcoholic, drinking to forget the atrocities he had witnessed in Dachau. Some had committed suicide so as not to crack under torture. But, there were others who had done little more than hide in the forest, and were still hailed as heroes when they came out after the war. This compared with the neglect of the war sailors, filled my father with rage and bitterness that remained with him for as long as he lived.

The Catastrophe. Friday, August 31st 1945

On August 31st the Herbrand is anchored in Portland, Maine, up the coast from Boston.

My father notes in his diary: *03.05, horrendous explosion in tank 1 and 2. Leif Johansen, Oskar Jacobsen and Gunnar Karlsen are missing.*

This explosion was extensively reported on the front page of the *Portland Evening Express* of August 31st, by a reporter strangely enough named Leonard Cohen like the singer/poet. My father kept the cutting in his trunk in the attic along with other memorabilia until he gave it to John who passed it on to me, yellow with age but the style is modern. There are two articles. I have excluded a few paragraphs that are either repetitious or of little interest to our story. Apart from that I have copied everything exactly as it was written. So here it is splashed all over the front page:

Head shot of my father, clean shaven, uniform cap on his head, wearing his uniform. There are three photos of the wreckage. Quote:

Three Missing In Tanker Blast

Estimated Damage At $100,000

Explosion Shakes Local Waterfront, Lights Harbour Area.

Two Tanks of 15,000-ton Ship Ripped Open As Fumes ignite During Cleaning Process; had Discharged 4,500,000-Gallon Cargo

By Leonard J. Cohen

Three seamen presumed dead today in a shattering explosion and fire which ripped open the foredeck of the Norwegian tanker Herbrand like a piece of tin. The blast occurred at 3.30am and the vessel swung anchor 300 yards off the Eastern Promenade only a few hours after it had discharged a cargo of more than 4,500,000 gallons of crude oil to the Portland Pipeline Company.

The only trace of the three missing sailors, said Commander F.B. Lincoln, USN, section of the Coast Guard Office, was a piece of flesh found on the afterdeck of the blackened and blistered ship. All indications were that the men were blasted to pieces by the terrific explosion which aroused Portland and South Portland residents from their beds in fear that an earthquake had occurred.

Navy sources estimated the blast damage at approximately $100,000. The explosion shook the waterfront and the ensuing fire illuminated the whole harbour.

The missing seamen were:

Boatswain Leif Johansen, 29, of Finneide, Norway;

Able seaman Oscar Jacobsen, 33, of Moss, Norway;

Able seaman Gunnar Karlsen, 20, of Alstahaug, Helgeland.

The ship carried a complement of 42 officers and men, some of whom were ashore at the time. Except for the missing men, none of those abroad were injured.

Occurring in the two forward tanks of the 15,000-ton vessel, which Capt. Kristoffer Hoddevik said were empty, the blast ripped open the fore-deck, peeling half of it back over the portside and twisting the other half straight up into the air. Plates on the port side were buckled and left sagging. One of the tanker's three-ton anchors was blown from the bow completely over the bridge and crashed forward of amidships. Coast Guard firefighters said that only the fact that the anchor crashed into a stanchion on the spar deck prevented it from breaking through the main deck. Had it plunged through the main deck into the tanks below, it would undoubt-edly have caused another explosion and fire, officers said. Fifty-one depth charges and ammunition housed in a gun locker within 30 feet of the blasted tanks escaped the explosion and fire. Two British Royal Navy gun-ners served aboard the tanker.

'Search proceeded for traces of the men, two of them were known to have been on the foredeck, the other unaccounted for', Captain Hoddevik said. Surviving members of the crew showed evidence of a severe shaking-up.

'Fumes in the tanks as the 650-foot vessel was being steamed out prepa-ratory to going into dry dock. Leaving free steam turned on, crew members quelled the flames in about half an hour', the captain said.

Although Captain Hoddevik declared he had not "the least idea" of the cause of the blast, coast guardsmen reported that the fumes ignited when an electric light bulb broke.

Immediately following the explosion two life boats were lowered from the stern of the ship, and about a dozen crew members and their dog mascot, Lassie, took to one of the life boats. They returned to the Herbrand about 3.30am.

Captain Hoddevik was unable to estimate damage to the vessel.

Escaping the blast were six crew members who had shore leave for the night. Crew members were fortunate, they pointed out, that their quar-ters where most of them were asleep were aft and away from the two tanks where the blast occurred.

The Herbrand had left the pipe line dock at 9.50pm Thursday, going to the anchorage where steaming out of the tanks was begun. The ship was scheduled to go 50 miles out to sea to pump oil residue from the tanks. After cleaning she was to go to dock to have her wartime spar deck burned off. The spar deck had been used for carrying supercargo during the war but was to be removed because the ship was in the process of transfer from the War Shipping Administration back to her owners.

Another article in the same paper:

Norwegian Crew Stunned By Ship's Postwar Tragedy.

By Franklin Wright.

Her entire forward section smashed and twisted by a fierce explosion, the Norwegian tanker Herbrand lay crippled in Portland Harbour today—and the 39 remaining members of her crew just couldn't understand why?

Was bound for home.

With a valiant record of service in every combat zone from the Persian Gulf to the Caribbean the Herbrand was going home. Why, asked the seamen, here at this peaceful anchorage did such a thing have to happen?

No one could answer their question as the crewmen gathered in little knots about the deck. Many of the men, still dazed from the shock of the blast, stood apart, reluctant to talk to anyone. Their voices dropped almost to whispers as they spoke of the three men working on that deck. 'Missing? That's a gentle word,' one seaman remarked as he overheard a reporter's question. 'There's no need to hunt for them', he added.

At the centre of one of the little groups of men was Olav Henriksen, a seaman from Nøtterøy, Norway. When the blast came he was working in one of the little summer tanks, immediately under the deck and over the main tanks. Miraculously he escaped uninjured.

What happened? 'I'll never know any more than those other boys. I was in the only one of those seven little tanks that did not explode. I was just working along when everything around me blew up and started to burn,' he said.

Another crewman who identifies himself only as Samuelsen again brought up the subject of the ironic twist of fate which seemed to have affixed itself to the ship.

Ex Underground Man killed.

'Gunnar Karlsen, one of the missing men, joined the ship in New York just a few days ago. He was only 20. All during the German occupation of Norway he had worked with the Underground. A few months ago the Germans had been as it was hot on his trail and he escaped from the country. After all those months of war, it seems odd that he should be taken in something like this,' Samuelsen said.

My father on the day following the explosion
(Photo Portland Evening Express, 1945)

I can't begin to think how terrible this must have been for my father. On the photo that was taken following the explosion he looks serious, sad, resigned—his eyes gazing out into the distance as though hoping that salvation and escape from the awful life he's living might be out there, beyond the horizon. How could this have happened in a safe harbour after the long years of dodging German U-boats, warships and bomber-planes on the open ocean?

His diary entries are even shorter and more to the point than usual, probably all he could bear to write. Handwriting almost illegible in places.

Sunday, September 2: *Pastor Thorvik conducted a funeral ceremony on board.*

September 3: *Inquiry with the Norwegian Vice Consul, the First Officer, the Third Officer and Jørgen Kristiansen.*

September 6: *Able Seaman Oskar Jakobsen found, dead. Mechanics on board regarding removal of wreckage.*

September 7, Friday: *Received gas-free certificate. Oskar Jakobsen's funeral.*

September 8, Saturday: *Boatswain Leif Johansen's funeral.*

He says nothing about the funeral of 20 year-old Gunnar Karlsen, so he must have been blown to such tiny pieces that there was nothing to find and nothing to bury.

September 10, Monday: *Workmen began removing the wreckage. Started on starboard deck. Workmen started removing the remnants of port side deck.*

September 12. *Handed in papers to the Vice Consul regarding the fatalities. Had conversation with the Consulate in New York.*

After this the entries are not very clear and it's difficult to make sense of them as it is mainly about technicalities. As far as I can gather he took his stricken ship to Boston for repairs.

On October 11th he checks in at the Lord Baltimore Hotel in New York. Not many entries after this, and they are all to do with work and administration. The entries seem low key, nothing about Ross or parties. The years at sea had not broken his spirit, but the explosion seems to have had a profound effect. And all the time there was business to attend to; he was the captain.

Nothing in his diary to mark 1945 passing into history. No entry at all, only a blank page. The year that started out with a festive dinner in the *Old English Tearoom* at the Prince George Hotel, seems to have fizzled out into a non-event not worth mentioning. And not a word about Ross.

On December 23rd he sends a telegram to my mother that simply says: *Merry Christmas and happy New Year. Regards Kristoffer.*

The Home Coming

For a long time I had no idea of my father's whereabouts during the first eight months of 1946 except that it was business as usual. All I knew was that one fine day in August 1946 he was back in Norway. Walking down the gangway of the ferry from Newcastle, he was carrying a huge bunch of bananas. The family had turned up in force to meet him. The bananas made a lasting impression; Auntie Marie talked about it for years. No banana had been seen in Norway since before the war and never a bunch that size.

Now, thanks to the Brazilian article that John found among his papers, I realize that this must have coincided with his time on the fruit boat, Atlantic Express. It certainly would explain the huge bunch of bananas. One may wonder why it took him more than a year of peacetime to get back to his family, but be that as it may.

People flew less in those days. The ferries were the main means of transport between Norway and the UK and between Norway and New York, for that matter: Newcastle—Kristiansand—Oslo, Oslo—Kristiansand—Newcastle. Newcastle—Bergen, Bergen—Newcastle. Backwards and forwards they went, sea often rough, people getting seasick.

In the 1950s my father often arrived on the Braemar. I remember it well. A day of celebration. All of us going by taxi to Oslo. Waiting on the quayside. Trying to spot Dad amongst the other passengers on deck leaning against the railings, ready to disembark. And there he was! The excitement as the gangway was lowered, and finally Dad walking down towards us, setting foot on dry land. John and I running up to meet him. The taxi ride home. The presents. The unfamiliar sweets. And Dad, white shirt, tie—smelling differently; tobacco, aftershave, foreign lands . . .

John remembers one such occasion. Seeing the ferry arriving he asked Mum: 'Where is England?' Mum pointed westwards and replied 'over there'. But over there, less than a mile away, was the green shore of Nesodden. John assumed it to be England and couldn't understand what all the fuss was about.

In 1946 this was still years into the future. There were no little children running up to meet him. Only my mother and Bjørn, nine years old, hair carefully combed, new tweed suit with short trousers—God knows where Mum had managed to get hold of the material as there was very little to be had in the shops . . . Anders and Marie, permanent fixtures whenever something was happening, invited or not. His sisters: Entse, Astrid and Petra, all qualified nurses. Bjørn; shy, quiet, knowing that this man, of whom he only had the haziest memory, was his father. The huge bunch of bananas . . .

Time drifts by, slipping through our fingers like water and sand, a well-worn cliché but I can't think of a better way of putting it. I was in Newcastle some 15 years ago, when Sam was 18, for an open day at Newcastle University. We took a taxi to the university. The driver wondered why we needed a taxi, it wasn't far at all. I replied: 'Maybe so, but we're a bit late and we can't afford to get lost'. The driver said all right then, but it really isn't very far. Whereupon he drove round a corner and up a hill and that was it.

Sam decided against Newcastle University and I never set foot in the city again.

Years passed between my father taking the ferry from Newcastle and me spending a day there whilst Sam was being shown round the university and interviewed. I like to think that we did walk some of the same streets, set eyes on the same sights. Lives touching briefly, paths crossing and nearly crossing with years and years in between.

Back to 1946. My father was brought back to a small and crummy first floor flat. A medium sized house one and a half stories high standing by itself in the middle of fields and surrounded by apple trees, at the end of the fields, the ever present forest, dark and oppressive. He never liked dense forests; they close in on you so you can hardly breathe. Anders and Marie downstairs, listening, hearing everything that went on upstairs. Bjørn, poor thing, grown up with shortages of every kind—seeing Anders, an uneducated smallholder and part-time labourer, as a father figure . . . Everybody loved Bjørn, a sensitive little boy, fond of flowers and animals but deeply entrenched in local life showing little interest in the wider world, never asking him about his ship or the countries that he had visited. He was intelligent, and his teacher was pleased with him, and he was popular with the other children. Kristoffer saw these qualities, but he couldn't help thinking that they were somehow wasted, that it was too late, that the boy had lived too long under the influence of a country bumpkin. He realised that his fantasies of sending Bjørn to boarding school in England were just that—fantasies. And Martha—her dark hair turned salt and pepper even if she was only 34. Threadbare clothes, no makeup, still attractive, he had to admit with her dark eyes and golden skin—until she opened her mouth and out came banalities about things local that didn't interest him or tales from the occupation that did, but only up to a point. Anecdotes that in no way could compare to the things he had seen and experienced. And, the dirty legacy of the Germans clinging to everything you set eyes on, the very fabric of the country permeated with their filthy presence—the jeeps and horses they had left behind, now appropriated by petty and opportunistic Norwegians. No decent food in the shops. Paint and plasterwork flaking off buildings, people looking grey and shabby, everything drab and desolate. No interesting people to talk to. Living in a cramped flat above Martha's brother and wife . . . They seemed to have adopted Bjørn, he spent more time with them than with his mother. And the two snotty Nazi brats that he played with, hanging around eying their food at mealtimes till he had to tell them to leave . . . He asked Martha how she could allow Bjørn to keep such company. Martha replied that she'd had no choice. She'd been worried that their father might find some reason to report her to the Gestapo and what would have become of Bjørn if she was taken away? Besides, it wasn't the boys' fault that their parents were traitors; given half a chance they could still turn into decent people.

He felt sorry for Martha. She'd been so delighted to see him again, had made a big effort with the flat, small as it was, the furniture wasn't bad and she had pictures on the walls and ornaments, fresh wild-flowers everywhere. But however hard he tried he just could not conceal his deep dislike for the drab and bleak country he had returned to. And to think that he could have taken Mr Laszinsky up on his offer and settled in Trinidad. That was at the end of 1944 when he'd had drinks with him in New York. Bjørn and Martha had hardly been part of the equation when he declined the offer. All he had thought was that he wouldn't have it said about him that he had disappeared ashore during the war, and so he signed on to the

G. C. Brøvig and set out on a gruelling North Atlantic crossing. He'd liked Mr Laszinsky, a second generation Polish immigrant. Like many North-East Europeans there was something solid and sincere about him. Any offer he made was bound to be genuine.

What riled him the most was that Anders was decorated for his resistance work—for smuggling dynamite to the 'boys in the forest' right under the very noses of the Germans. He didn't begrudge Anders his medal. He had put his life on the line and deserved the recognition. But what about him and all the other sailors who had been risking their lives, every day for years? Didn't they deserve a medal as well? Besides, the people in the resistance could flee to Sweden or England if the Germans got too hot on their heels, and many of them did. Many got caught of course, and sent to Germany and some never returned. He wasn't belittling their bravery. But there were also those who had done precious little apart from hiding in the forest, and still were given a hero's welcome when they ventured out into the open. The crew of a tanker or ammunition ship in the middle of the ocean had no option but to stay put. They could jump ship once they got to a harbour, but somehow few of them did. He had been to Oslo and seen the plight of some of the seamen. Seen them sleeping in shacks and under bridges because they had no money and no home or family to return to. People said they were tramps and drunks, but then again—who wouldn't seek refuge in a bottle when that was their only escape and they knew that each day might be their last.

And the worst ignominy of all: When he needed his passport renewed he'd gone along to the police station in Hønefoss in good faith thinking that it was only a formality. Instead he'd been met by a baby-faced 18-year-old who asked him for documentation as to his political stance during the war. In other words proof that he had not been a collaborator. That was when he exploded: 'How can I have bloody been a collaborator after serving my country at sea for six years transporting oil for the British so they could win the war! I'm not going to give you proof of anything! Call my Head Office if you like! Where is your boss? I want to see your boss'. The terrified youth disappeared soon after to return with an older policeman: 'And what seems to be the problem?'

'The problem is that after serving my country for six years as the captain of an oil tanker I'm being asked to submit proof that I have not been a collaborator.'

125

'Don't take it personally. It's just something we have to ask everybody who claims to have returned from the sea. Otherwise, how can we know what they were really up to, but I can assure you that in your case it's only a formality'.

Kristoffer was about to tell him to stick his passport where the sun doesn't shine, but managed to bite his tongue. No point in arguing with rules and bureaucracy. He needed his passport if he was to continue working. So he summoned up his dignity, calmly put his old passport and new photo on the counter, scribbled down the phone number of his Head Office and said: 'There you are. Do ring them up. I think you will find that my war record is impeccable, and let me know when my passport is ready for collection.' With that he turned on his heel and left.

He was so furious that he had to go to Café Ciro for a beer to calm down, a miserable joint it was too, the haunt of alkies and youths with no money but what else was there in this god-forsaken town.

To have something to read on the bus home he bought a local paper. Plastered all over the front page was a large photo and interview with a 15-year-old schoolboy. His father had been in the resistance, and the boy had sneaked coded messages into his Norwegian essays for his teacher, also in the resistance, to pick up. An act of bravery as many of the teachers at the school had been Nazis. For this the boy had been decorated and had his photo and interview all over the front page. Nobody had asked him or any other sailor that he knew of for an interview. Kristoffer was seething with anger. Was this boy so much braver than other boys, not much older than him, who had witnessed men torched and blown to bits and still stayed the course! Or for that matter, was he so much braver than hundreds of captains like himself who had stood on the bridge for days on end, dodging torpedoes and had been in open combat with German war-ships and bomber planes! And don't give him the rubbish that the sailors did what they did because it was their job and they had no choice. There was a choice. They could have gone ashore, but for reasons only known to themselves they did not. As for him, he could have left his ship and started a comfortable life with Mr Laszinsky in Trinidad. Mr Laszinsky had given him a good offer. After he'd declined Mr Laszinsky had even got back to him a couple of months later and asked if he had changed his mind.

Anders had been awarded a medal. The schoolboy and God knows who else had been given medals. Kristoffer wasn't saying it was unmerited. But didn't he and other captains and the thousands of ordinary sailors deserve a token of gratitude as well? Instead it was business as usual for the captains and a hard and cold bed under a bridge for many sailors.

Another thing that he found strangely disappointing, the icing on a drab and tasteless cake so to speak, was that the story of the driver who drove a busload of Germans into the abyss, killing himself and them in the process, turned out not to be true. He'd asked local people about it, hoping to find out more detail, that they might have known the driver, but they had never heard about it. It hadn't happened, just a legend born out of wishful thinking, or a case of Chinese whispers, one feather becoming three hens, as they say.

He very much wanted to build a house near his parents' farm in the West Country. But Martha said that no way was she moving to that horrible treeless place with nothing but mountains and freezing winds and the sea. Besides what about Bjørn who was happy and settled here? And her parents—they were getting on and she was the only daughter living close by. And so it was decided that they would buy a piece of land from Anders, a useless piece as far as farming was concerned, but the position was good, on a hill overlooking the lake and the distant mountains. He had enough money put by, plus the money from the Nortraship Fund. They were dragging their feet about paying it. The sailors, himself included, had expected a bank draft as soon as the war was over but he realised that this had been over-optimistic. Distributing such a large sum fairly and squarely to so many people wasn't done overnight.

He stayed with Martha and Bjørn for a few weeks during which they all visited his family in the West Country, to a hero's welcome. Nobody else from that tiny place had achieved what Kristoffer had achieved in his life. His status was legendary and people came flocking from far and wide to see him.

* * *

The dreamy landscape father that my father failed to engage with.
A corner of the house on the left.

In the early summer of 1947 he was back and the building of his dream house got under way. It wasn't easy, as building materials such as cement and good wood were expensive and hard to come by. This time he and Bjørn travelled to the West Country without Martha. By the time he left for the Sea, school had started and Bjørn wrote a long essay about his journey making it into a real adventure. It seemed he'd got a lot out of his holiday. Kristoffer was pleased when he read it. The new house was taking shape. No turrets, but grand all the same. The black shiny roof-tiles that he had envisaged were nowhere to be found, so he had to make do with ordinary terracotta. Martha was pregnant—new life in a day and age he hadn't seriously believed he would live to see. Being in Norway wasn't so bad after all. Or was it? People looked at the house he was building and whispered: *Too big and pretentious ... All right for some, having made tons of money while other people were starving ...* Martha being excluded when neighbouring women got together for a coffee. Kristoffer noticed it all and it upset him more than he cared to admit. Martha pretending that the neighbours were gossips and fishwives that she wanted nothing to do with . . . No recognition and being ostracized into the bargain. Why on earth had he given in to Martha and agreed to settle in this out-of-the-way place with its small-minded and envious people. But Martha's parents, Maren and Johan, were loyal. He liked them. Maren was a plump little woman with her hair in a bun who always had some treat or other in her larder. Martha's father was handsome, almost military-looking with his hooked nose, thick white hair and dark eyes, a smallholder who supplemented his income by fishing in the lake and selling his catch in the market in Hønefoss. By being more enterprising than most, his family had always had what they needed even in the meagre 1930s when many people could barely eat. When neighbours commented to him: 'Your son-in-law is building quite a mansion isn't he?' Old Johan would hear the sarcasm in their voices and reply: 'Don't worry, he's got enough money put by to build one more the same.' On Sunday mornings Kristoffer would get on his bike, literally, and spend a couple of hours with his in-laws. Their home, a white wooden house with fretwork around roof-ridge and windows, was small but with a large veranda surrounded by a lush garden. When Kristoffer arrived, Johan would go to the spring behind the house where he had a couple of beers cooling in the water and so they would sit on the veranda, enjoying their beer and talking about not very much.

The Nortraship money looked unlikely to materialize. Now they were saying that it was only to go to needy sailors and the families of sailors that had perished. Fair enough, but what about the sailors who had counted on the money, the houses they were planning to build, the cars they hoped to buy, helping younger siblings get started, or simply rebuilding their lives. Oh, they had been looking forward to this money, if only they survived the war, but instead they got nothing, zilch, nada. And what about the poor sods sleeping under bridges in Oslo and other cities, incapacitated mentally or physically, often both! Shouldn't they have had their fair share of the money ages ago? The authorities and with them the Seamen's Union had a ready answer: The sailors had only been doing their job and didn't deserve any special reward; before the war they had been keen to help their country and thus agreed to the salary reduction. Of course they wanted to help their country, but when they agreed to the salary reduction it was because they had been given to believe that the difference would be paid out to them after the war. But now the authorities and with them the Seamen's Union were adamant that the sailors had not actually been promised the money. Thus the Seamen's Union was going against its own members! How could that be? In short, the sailors didn't deserve anything, not even a lousy medal for staying the course and that at a time when medals were handed out left, right and centre. Like the 15-year old schoolboy. Was he so much more deserving than the youngsters who had been separated from their families for years knowing they might be blown up at any minute! More deserving than that poor boy, Andreas Vik his name was, that they had pulled from a lifeboat one sunshiny summer's night up in the Barents Sea, barely conscious, his skin burnt, his lips cracked and swollen after more than a week in the lifeboat. His mate, not much older than him and in almost the same condition, helping to lift his friend to his feet so the men from the Herbrand could hoist him up the ladder. The other men in the lifeboat were beyond saving. Kristoffer had concocted a solution of water, salt and sugar for the boys to drink. Their condition had soon improved and after a couple of days they were laughing and joking, eager to help out with whatever needed doing. But where were they now? Perished in another torpedo attack, or sleeping under a bridge? Hopefully they'd had good homes to return to. But even so—the injustice of it all was horrendous.

The 1950s and beyond

After the war my father was back circumnavigating the world—the Indian Ocean, down to Australia, through the Suez Canal in peace time, around the Cape of Good Hope during the Suez crises. He sailed to China where he bought me pyjamas of thick white silk with embroidered roses in red and pink. He visited Japan where he bought pearls (a necklace, studs and a ring) for my mother. He brought us large colourful silk scarves, not the sort you'd wear in Norway, so both scarves remained in my chest of drawers. Once in a while I took them out to contemplate their texture and beauty. One was bright red, the other one blue and white with a giant peacock. The red one I think had an image of the Taj Mahal. I had never heard about the Taj Mahal back then so I cannot be certain, but that's what I remember.

He even sailed up to the frosty North. There was his over-night docking at Fagerstrand near Oslo when we all stayed the night on his ship. Once he was in Stockholm where Mum and John spent a few days with him. I was in a critical year at school and had to stay behind with Bjørn and Randi. As if a few days' absence would have ruined exams that were still months away! It was wintertime and during the day John watched the ice-breakers on the Baltic. There was a beautiful young radio operator on board and John was so mesmerized by her that once he burnt his mouth on the soup. All this and more while I was sitting at home and going to school. Imagine what I could have soaked up in historic Stockholm, staying on an oil tanker, gaining insight into my father's life. They went shopping in Stockholm's department stores and bought me a necklace that I've still got

131

and lovely mohair material that Mum fashioned into a dress for me. Still, hardly a substitute for a glimpse of the wider and more interesting world. Instead it was endless lessons with our boring old teacher, Mr Frohaug, who was pushing seventy. He did a good job of teaching us maths, spelling and grammar, but firing our imagination and widening our horizons was not is forte.

My first memory of my father? Our property was surrounded by the enormous Northern forests that one way or another stretch all the way to the Pacific via Sweden, Finland, European Russia and Siberia. In fact we owned a miniscule corner of it; five tall spruces and some bushes and undergrowth. Dad was making a small wooden gate in the fence between our property and the rest of the forest. I was with him and I was two and a couple of months old. Dad had finished the gate and wanted to go back inside. I didn't want to. I had never been to the edge of the forest before and I loved it, the coolness, the tall grass, the large pale-blue flowers, taller than me—watching Dad shaping the wood with his axe . . . I refused to leave and was on the ground kicking and screaming. Dad lifted me up and carried me towards the house. I kicked and screamed even more tearing at his hair and scratching his face. It was no use. We were back at the house. Mum was there. She said: 'You're a bad girl, look, Dad's got no hair now, you've torn it all out'. I stopped fighting then. It was true. The top of Dad's head was completely clean, not a hair. I really had been bad. For years I believed that Dad was bald because I had pulled out his hair that day in the forest.

But then he disappeared. Dad was at sea. That was all there was to it. At home were Mum, Bjørn and I. When John came along there were four of us, and subsequently, after Bjørn had married and moved out there were Mum, John and I. There was an interlude when Bjørn and his family lived with us but after a few months they moved into their own house and the uneventful days continued. But then Dad came home and everything livened up and changed. Aunties and uncles and people I didn't know came to visit. Dad brought home exciting and unusual things, colourful rugs, an Arabic fez, a life-size walking doll for me called Diana, a toy tank firing shells and blowing smoke for John, a stuffed baby crocodile that he said he'd shot, but nobody believed him. And above all sweets, unfamiliar sweets, not like the ones we could buy in Norway. Sweets were the greatest treat. Mum only allowed us one bar of chocolate on Saturdays. She couldn't see the point in wasting good money on things that would only rot our teeth.

Me, one year old in a dress that my father had bought in Italy.
I've still got the cross.

When did I become Daddy's girl? Difficult to say. John was born when I was three and Mum was busy with him most of the time. He cried a lot and there was often something wrong with him. Grandma and Grandpa would pop in or we'd call on them. Grandma often had my favourite dish ready, vanilla blancmange with crushed almonds. She made me a seal out of black fluffy material. I called him Snorre Seal and carried him with me everywhere. What became of him I don't know. Most likely Mum chucked him out when he'd got worn and grubby. But few episodes in my early years stand out except when Dad was home on leave.

I don't know when it first dawned on me that we weren't very popular. We were on the periphery of things. I noticed other women chattering and talking to each other at the bus stop, but Mum stood apart, aloof, an outsider in her elegant dress with matching shoes, handbag and hat. There were times when she was not on speaking terms with her siblings. I remember when her sister, Johanna, arrived from Stockholm staying with their parents. She never visited us, nor did we go to see Grandma and Grandpa while she was there. I sensed that we were unpopular because we had a bigger house than most, and a car. And what a car it was! An enormous green Dodge with room for seven people; bought second-hand and shipped over from America. Such things were not tolerated in egalitarian post-war Norway where people were encouraged to be as alike as possible. This stems partly from a shortcoming in the Norwegian language where the word for equality 'likhet' means both equality as in 'equal rights' and 'sameness' and it was the latter meaning that became the accepted interpretation in Norway: Everybody should be the same. Having money, possessions, talent, beauty or a shining personality was only tolerated as long as you kept it under wraps and pretended you didn't have it—i.e. that you were exactly like everyone else. I remember Christmas parties at school when I was scorned for having a new dress:

'So you've got a new dress this year as well, you had a new one last year too, I have the same dress as last year, I do.'

'And so have I,' another girl chipped in self-righteous and pleased with herself, 'my mum says we don't all have bags of money'.

I never told Mum about things like this. Her parents had not been well off. She had craved new and pretty clothes, something to be proud of, but been forced to wear Johanna's cast-offs instead. Grandpa was strict: 'These are good clothes, nothing wrong with them.' So, she had promised herself that if she ever had a daughter she would make sure that she always looked smarter than the rest. Mum never found out that I had to endure snide remarks each time I came to school in something nice and new, Norwegian children don't wear school-uniforms. Still, her legacy has remained with me. I have always been fastidious about my appearance. Even when the boys were young and I didn't have two pennies to rub together I somehow managed to look reasonably smart—cheap and cheerful; bright T-shirts, Indian skirts, red, yellow or green trousers . . . I knitted jumpers for the boys and myself. Mum would knit for us too and sometimes she sent me money ordering me to buy something to wear. Friends sometimes gave me things they had no use for. A straight skirt of purple velvet that a neighbour had made for her daughter springs to mind. Her daughter didn't like it, so our neighbour gave it to me. I loved that skirt and wore it till it barely hung together. This threadbare existence continued for about fifteen years. In the mid-1980s Maher's salary increased. I made more money from freelance jobs and writing. I got a nice sum when my father passed away. Gradually our standard of living improved and we could afford a few frivolities to brighten our lives.

In my class there was one girl, Unni, who did not like me and I never found out why. She was the daughter of Mum's childhood neighbour, Thora, who had been a Nazi and worked for the Germans during the war. At the day of reckoning Thora was taken to court and given a five months' prison sentence for collaboration. I remember my mother's exact words: "Because she was pregnant they let her off till she'd had the baby and stopped breast feeding, but then she had to serve her sentence." That baby was Unni. She would stick her tongue out at me when nobody was looking. However, overweight and pallid, she was hardly the queen of the playground so this didn't really bother me. In fact she was a bit of a laughing stock, mainly on account of her essays. Our class consisted of 13 boys and girls. Every week Mr Frohaug made us read our essays out loud after he had marked them. The subjects were of the kind 10—11-year olds write about: *A day I'll never forget, My birthday, What I did during half term,* and so on. But, whatever the heading Unni managed to twist it so that she ended up writing about cakes and baking.

Thora's brother, Thorleif, who'd been a more passive kind of Nazi, and got off with a suspended sentence, developed serious mental problems, went stark raving mad in fact. These days with political correctness and improved psychological knowledge we would call it schizophrenia and psychotic episodes. Like the winter when I was nine and God had told him to build affordable houses all over Norway. I remember it clearly because he didn't have a telephone, not everybody did back then, so he would come to us to order materials for his building projects. For example; God had told him to order fifty telephones and five hundred typewriters, which he would need for his nationwide business. Dad was away and Mum was alone with John and me. Bjørn had moved out. This coming and going of his went on for ten days or so. At first Mum felt sorry for him, they had grown up together, but as he became more hateful towards people who'd tried to talk sense into him, banging the table and screaming that he wanted to kill them, looking unkempt with the madman's glint in his eyes getting increasingly frightening, she became terrified of him. Marie kept an eye out and when he came, she would soon arrive under some pretext. Still, she couldn't always be there. One night we made sure all doors were locked, turned off the lights and hid upstairs in Mum's bedroom so that if he came, he would think we'd gone out. The only light that had been left on was a bedside lamp. And there we sat hardly daring to breathe, on the floor, lest he should see our silhouettes through the blinds. And he came, suddenly there was banging on the front door. It continued for some time, but finally it stopped. Mum peeped out through a slit between the blind and the wall and saw him walking off down the passage. Goes without saying, we didn't venture downstairs again that night and eventually we fell asleep in the darkened house. All the neighbours knew what was going on with him. In fact they talked about little else. They realised that he might be a real danger to other people and he was sectioned and locked up in a padded cell. He never fully recovered and the rest of his life was spent in and out of psychiatric institutions until he passed away in the mid-1960s. His wife survived him many years but kept to herself. Their two sons, Arne and Anton, became decent men. Arne took himself off to technical college in Stockholm, married and had two or three children. Anton was very shy and spent most of his life working as a miner in Northern Norway. He never married and now lives on his own at the edge of the forest, a bit of a hermit really. He was in his late teens when his father went mad and it affected him badly. Over the years he has become more sociable. I often talk to him when I'm in Norway. He has a beautiful smile and offers me a lift if he happens by when I'm walking to or from Sundvollen.

As for Unni, I have no idea what became of her. I have asked people I went to school with but nobody seems to know.

We didn't live in total isolation. Auntie Astrid would come up from Oslo about once a month. We saw Auntie Entse and her husband, Uncle Arne, every fortnight or so. Uncle Arne was a wonderful man. Being childless he and Entse doted on John and me. They made puppet theatres for us, told us fairy-tales and took us to the park in Hønefoss, where they lived, to see the ducks and swans. But then everything changed. Mum's parents passed away much too soon, Grandma when I was five and Grandpa when I was eight. At around the same time Auntie Entse and Uncle Arne moved to Halden, a small town by the Swedish border. We only saw them 3—4 times a year after that. To cap it all, Bjørn married and moved out shortly before I was nine.

So there we lived, Mum, John and I in our large house on the hill, alone, the people that used to be around suddenly gone. Even Auntie Astrid's visits grew less frequent. Apart from two boys, John's age, there were no other children close by. Every so often Anne-Lise, my oldest friend in the whole world, and her brother, Einar, would visit their grandparents who lived next door and we'd play with them, except when Mum had been quarrelling with their mother or grandmother, quarrels that invariably ended with Mum telling John and me never to talk to those children ever again. John, being an obedient little boy, would do as he was told, whereas I would sneak across the fence next time they came to visit. John would follow suit. By then Mum would have calmed down sufficiently to let us get on with it. In summer two sisters my age, Lisbeth and Anne, would come up from the city and spend their holidays in their cabin by the forest. They were my summer friends and we spent our days swimming and rowing around the lake. School was a two kilometre-walk and a bus-ride away and so made it hard to meet up with classmates afterwards, which didn't really bother me as I never felt truly part of their games and whispered secrets. I was happier on my own, reading or drawing and listening to the radio; they played a lot of classical music in those days. However, this doesn't mean that I didn't often feel lonely and isolated.

And so the years of my childhood went by, only punctuated by my father's return every second summer and my mother's quarrels with family and neighbours, rows born out of jealousy and mutual dislike, aggravated by my mother's temper and refusal to let the smallest slight pass. To me the quarrels were extra painful because they intensified my sense of isolation. They would blow over, and we'd be back on speaking terms for a while, but I never knew how long it would last.

One of Dad's home comings sticks in my mind. I was nine or ten so John must have been around seven. We still had the large green Dodge. Bjørn was sometimes allowed to drive it when Dad was out at sea. Mum never learnt to drive. It was a Saturday in April and Dad was coming home. The sun shone from a blue sky and most of the snow had melted away. John and I were hanging around bored, waiting for it to be time to go and pick up Dad from the airport. Anne-Lise and Einar were there but we didn't feel like playing. All of us hanging about outside in the sun, as

Norwegian children do. So there we were, listless, waiting for the day to pass. And finally it did. Mum called us in and we washed and changed into our good clothes.

Bjørn and Randi, John and I set off for the airport, Mum stayed home to prepare the meal. The drive took around 45 minutes. We passed the house of a girl in my class. She was outside with a couple of other children, her mother standing in the doorway wearing an apron and with a white dishcloth in her hands. Nearing the airport we drove past some large blocks of flats. I noticed a young woman with brown hair by her kitchen window. How I pitied the poor people who were only having an ordinary Saturday! Then we passed some large greenhouses and handsome villas. A plane was coming in for landing. Was it Dad's? There weren't that many planes back then. We left the main road that continued into Oslo. Soon we were at the airport, parked and entered the arrival hall. Bjørn found out that Dad's plane had landed a bit early. And there we stood, waiting, watching the passengers emerging through the swing doors, some received with hugs and kisses, others leaving quickly on their own. The stream of people thinned and stopped. And there we stood, despondent, hoping for a straggler and that the straggler would be Dad, but nobody emerged. What had happened? Hadn't Dad been on the plane? Bjørn went to inquire. Dad's name was on the passenger list, so where had he got to? We couldn't understand it. Hadn't we been waiting and watching since the first passengers appeared? I think Bjørn phoned Mum from a public telephone to tell her what had happened, but perhaps not, my memory is hazy. At any rate, Dad hadn't turned up and there was nothing else for it but to drive back home empty handed. By the time we reached the drive to our house it was dark. Bjørn spotted him first. 'There he is!' And there he was, large as life, in the dining room window, white shirt and tie, tall and solid, looking straight at us. No sooner had Bjørn parked the car than I ran inside and threw myself in his arms, my head only reaching his chest, a big strong man smelling of foreign lands, tobacco and aftershave. My dad.

Turned out he had been the first to get off the plane and as luck would have it, the first to retrieve his luggage. After that he had simply found a taxi and gone home, most likely getting into the taxi as we were entering the airport building. Communications were not the same then as now. He would send a telegram saying; arriving at such and such time at . . . either by ferry from England or by plane from wherever. We always came to meet him so what had possessed him to simply go off instead of waiting to see if we turned up?

When he came home he told stories, things that had happened to him since we last saw him. For example there was the time when he wiped the floor with lawyers and judges in an Australian court room. I think it happened in Kwinana, a god-forsaken little town with nothing much more than a few oil tanks: A young sailor had gone on shore leave and got drunk, as young sailors often do. In his drunken state he had somehow got into a parked car, but he hadn't managed to start it. The police found him in the car, slumped over the wheel, brought him to the station and locked him up for the night. The following day, he was up in court accused of breaking into a car with intent of stealing it; and facing a prison sentence if found guilty. My father had been alerted and turned up in the court room to represent him. Having heard how they had found the young man in the car my father asked the policeman who had arrested him:

'How did the young man react when you caught him?'

Police officer: 'He didn't react, he was paralytic.'

My father: 'Would you say that he was so paralytic that he was actually unconscious?'

Police officer: 'Yes, you could say that.'

My father: 'But can you really accuse an unconscious man of stealing a car?'

Silence in the court room. Case dismissed.

Back on the ship the young man thanked my father for having come to his rescue saying: 'God knows what would have become of me if I had ended up in prison in this dump.'

Another young sailor, Torgrim Lie, was in bed with severe stomach pains and vomiting. My father had a look at him and felt pretty sure it was appendicitis. He ordered him to stay in bed and told another young sailor to sit with him and on no account leave him alone. A few hours later the young man looking after Torgrim Lie knocked on my father's door and said: 'Torgrim wants to get up now because he feels a lot better.'

My father immediately knew what must have happened; the appendix had ruptured, spilling pus into the gut. When the appendix ruptures, the pressure is released and the excruciating pain is gone. My father told the boy to make sure his friend stayed in bed and to remain by his side.

Whereupon he changed course and went full steam to the nearest port where Torgrim was rushed to hospital and his life saved in the nick of time.

There were many such stories but these are two that spring to mind.

With Dad at home for the summer we invariably drove to visit his family in the West Country. Everything packed into the Dodge, Mother and Father in the front, John and I in the back. Sometimes Auntie Astrid would come with us as well. The journeys had a pattern. Driving to Lillehammer, stopping to buy food for lunch, which invariably meant potatoes and either frankfurters or a large tin of meat balls in gravy. Outside Lillehammer we would stop at a picnic site. John and I were dispatched to fetch water from a stream. Dad would light the little portable gas cooker. Mum would unpack the camping case which had everything we needed: two fold up chairs, for Mum and Dad, John and I would sit on a blanket. A dinner/lunch set of yellow plastic consisting of four cups, four plates and four knives, forks and spoons. Dad would relax with his pipe whilst Mum did the cooking. Basic as they were I still think of these meals as the best ever—the boiled potatoes tasting of peat and forest, the fried frankfurters slightly burnt on account of it being difficult to regulate the gas and the meatballs tasting better than Mum's own. And for desert—a handful of wild blueberries or raspberries that John and I had picked whilst waiting for the food . . .

Children complain about the boredom of long car journeys. John and I were never bored. Mum and Dad didn't go in for silly guessing games or any such pass-times to alleviate the monotony. We knew every kiosk along the way and at which kiosk we'd stop for an ice cream or a hotdog. John and I watched the landscape as it changed from fertile farmland to forest to naked mountain and eternal snow. If we came across a flock of goats on summer pasture we had to get out and stroke them feeding them whatever biscuits or snacks we had at hand. The mountain pass was a different world, barren, nothing could grow there, only grey naked rock interlaced with little lakes and rivers of green glacier water. Some years the snow was piled up two meters high along the road, other years there was less of it, but always snow, and never far from the road. We had to stop to walk on the snow, rough and grainy with cold wintry air rising from it. At Videseter, from where the road descends in sharp hairpin bends towards the Stryn Valley, we had to get out and look at the spectacular waterfall. Not only that; it was amazing to stand—snow on all sides, and look at the green and fertile valley below with its long narrow lake. Half way down we crossed

Europe's highest bridge. In the gorge deep below we could glimpse the white swirling river that a few minutes ago had been a fearsome waterfall. I wondered how they'd managed to build the bridge and if anyone had fallen in and got killed.

The journey took two days. These days there are tunnels so people make it on one. They call it progress—getting from A to B as quickly as possible to save a day or a few hours into which they can cram something else. On this route it means missing one of the most spectacular mountain passes in the world. Whizzing through a tunnel with their children plugged into some electronic game lest they get bored—knowing nothing of the glories above them.

In the early years we spent the night in a classy mountain lodge, later on, when our finances became more restricted, we stayed in Bed and Breakfasts in the Stryn Valley.

Dad may have been a hero of world's oceans, dodging submarines and warships, but a man of every-day practicalities he was not. It never occurred to him to give the Dodge a thorough overhaul before setting out on a major journey. Having made it across the mountains the old Dodge had usually had enough, and stopped. Once the breaks gave in just as we had finished the hairpin bends down towards Stryn, and we nearly ended up in the lake. Or something else went wrong and Mum, John and I had to continue by bus whilst Dad stayed with the car waiting for a spare part to arrive. When the engine stopped he would get out and open the bonnet. No idea what to look for. Sooner or later a kind driver would come by and sort out the problem, unless something was broken and we needed a spare part. And that was not all. Dad was better at navigating the Seven Seas than the winding mountain roads of Norway. I can hardly recall one journey when we didn't bump into another car or end up in a ditch or among the bushes. The Dodge was too large for the narrow roads of the time. Besides, Dad was heavy on the gas and liked to drive faster than the roads would allow.

One episode stands out. I remember it because it was such a lovely break in our journey and totally unexpected. We had made a detour that summer taking the ferry along the spectacular Gerianger Fjord, now visited by cruise ships from all over the world. By this time the green Dodge had been replaced by a yellow Vauxhall. We had completed the 50 hairpin bends from Hellesylt at the end of the Geiranger Fjord to the mountain plateau upon which the engine died. Dad jumped out and opened the bonnet. No clue what to look for. A car stopped and a man got out asking what the problem was. Dad had no idea. The man had a look and established that the fan-belt had snapped. Did we have a spare one? Of course not, dad had never heard of such a thing. John remembers that the man was Swedish and that he offered to give us a spare fan-belt that he had, but it didn't fit. So, Dad had to hitch a lift back down to Hellesylt hoping to find a garage where he could buy a fan-belt whilst Mum, John and I remained by the car. A beautiful warm afternoon, sun shining, the three of us pottering about, sitting on the dry ground soaking up the sun. The smell of warm heather, insects buzzing, and lemmings—hundreds of them scuttling about wherever we looked, so tiny and cute with their yellow stripes. Mum said that it must be a lemming-year, that every few years inexplicably huge numbers of lemmings are born, and then to regulate their numbers, they all jump off a cliff. John and I had never heard about this so we felt lucky to have witnessed it, even if we had our doubts about the mass-suicide. Finally Dad returned. He had managed to hitch a ride back up and he had the fan belt. The man who had given him the lift fitted the belt, and we were on our way.

In those days Western Norway was fanatically teetotal. Not a drop of alcohol to be had anywhere except in some of the main towns. Having arrived at our Bed and Breakfast after a day's driving Dad would invariably say: 'What wouldn't I give for a cold beer . . .' But to bring a couple of bottles and cool them in the washbasin in the bedroom . . . never thought of it. And neither did we.

These days the mantra seems to be: If you want to be a survivor in a changing world; then live in the present, think of the future and don't dwell on the past. True. But equally, we must keep open the channels to our history, to our roots, to who we are, for what are we if not the sum of our memories, sounds banal but it's true. Our memories are the treasures of our lives like ancient cloth and beautiful artefacts which although faded and worn retain a patina that no new object straight from the shop can compete with.

You may say that the recollections I have written down are not that special, no great drama, no earth-shattering tragedy, no abuse or incest, so obligatory these days in any self-respecting memoir. Maybe so. Then again it is not the experience per se that is important, more significant is who you share it with and how it affects you. When a distant relative in the West Country posted a photo of my father's village on Face Book, John commented: "The green valley of my childhood".

One more memory, or rather a cluster of memories are engraved in my mind. We lived two kilometres, about one and a quarter mile, from Sundvollen (now known because of its proximity to the atrocity on Utøya). The main road linking Oslo to Hønefoss and continuing up country towards the North and the West passes through Sundvollen. A less important road runs along the opposite side of the lake and past our house, but the busses on that side were irregular, and never after 8.30pm, too early for a girl in her late teens/early 20s. Walking the two kilometres to or from Sundvollen in full daylight was never a problem, except if I had a lot to carry. But, a long stretch of the road runs through a forest of dense dark fir trees, fine during the day, but frightening at night with the trees closing in; pitch black, not a light or a house in sight. Walking through the forest after dark used to terrify me, still does. Anything could be lurking behind the trees—wolves, ghosts, aliens . . . Or, a car might come by with the type of man you really don't want to meet alone, on a deserted road . . . Consequently I would ring Dad and tell him when I'd be arriving in Sundvollen so he could pick me up. And pick me up he did. However late or come rain, shine or snow-storm. Dad would be there, waiting at the bus stop with King, his golden Labrador who came with him wherever he went. The yellow Vauxhall had given way to a black Austin Cambridge, the last car Father ever bought and which he drove almost till his dying day at the age of 81.

In my mind the innumerable times he picked me up have fused in to one enduring memory: Late afternoon, blue sky, sunshine, early autumn, leaves beginning to change from green to orange. Bus stopping, me getting out with my bits and pieces. Dad waiting at the bus stop wearing his grey and green checked shirt and old charcoal trousers, black beret on his head. King by his side, excited, waiting, jumping for joy when he sees me. Behind them long autumn grass and slightly further away the black Austin Cambridge.

If only I could turn back the clock.

A moment in time. My father and Sam (15months old) in the garden. They were sitting like that for ages.

The Albatross

An albatross aloft can be a spectacular sight. These feathered giants have the longest wingspan of any bird—up to 11 feet (3.4 meters)! The wandering albatross is the biggest of some two dozen different species. Albatrosses use their formidable wingspans to ride the ocean winds and sometimes to glide for hours without rest or even a flap of their wings. They also float on the sea's surface, though that position makes them vulnerable to aquatic predators. Albatrosses drink salt water, as do some other sea birds. Some albatross species were heavily hunted for feathers that were used as down and in the manufacture of women's hats.

These birds have reached a documented 50 years of age. They are rarely seen on land and gather only to breed, at which time they form large colonies on remote islands. Mating pairs produce a single egg and take turns caring for it. Young albatrosses may fly within three to ten months, depending on the species, but then leave the land behind for some five to ten years until they themselves reach sexual maturity. Some species appear to mate for life.

Albatrosses feed primarily on squid or schooling fish, but are familiar to mariners because they sometimes follow ships in the hope of dining on hand-outs or garbage. Albatrosses have a special place in maritime lore and superstition, most memorably evoked in Samuel Taylor Coleridge's *The Rime of the Ancient Mariner* about how a Ship having passed the Line was driven by storms to the cold country towards the South Pole.

At length did cross an Albatross,
Through the fog it came;
As if it had been a Christian soul,
We hailed it in God's name.
It ate the food it ne'er had eat,

And round and round it flew.
The ice did split with a thunder-fit;
The helmsman steered us through!
And a good south wind sprung up behind;
The Albatross did follow,
And every day, for food or play,
Came to the mariner's hollo!

Tank Empress, Late 1950s

September. Autumn in Norway, spring in Southern Africa. Spring, new life on the open sea after two claustrophobic months with Martha and the kids. Kids . . . he is 56 for God's sake. Men his age are supposed to be grandfathers not the fathers of young children. Well, he is a grandfather too. Bjørn—he had high hopes for him, and the boy is handsome, dark-haired and dark-eyed like his mother, intelligent, full of humour, well-liked by everybody. But he doesn't seem to have any ambition apart from being an ordinary person out in the sticks where he grew up, no desire to make something of his life. Not like him and his sisters. And then he took up with a girl, Randi, when he was 18. Randi is good-looking, tall and well-dressed with brown hair and green eyes; he understands that Bjørn could fall in love with her. Decent but ordinary family, no particular ambition, and like Bjørn—the older of much younger siblings. After a year of going out together Randi fell pregnant and they got married. A father at 19 . . . not what Kristoffer had in mind for him. Anders gave them a piece of land as a wedding present and Bjørn, poor thing, is working day and night, first his apprenticeship in Oslo, he's training to be an electronics engineer, and then spending his evenings and weekends working on the house they are building. In the meantime Martha has taken them in. What else could she do? She and little Margrethe are looking after one-year-old Rune while Randi goes to work in the little supermarket in Sundvollen.

Kristoffer is glad to be back at sea. There was no peace in the house. Margrethe or Meea, as she prefers to be called, seemed nervous and edgy. She spent very little time at home, either she was going for walks with

147

Rune in his pushchair, or she was by the lake swimming with her friends. John spent most of his time reading Disney comics. There was no place for Kristoffer in the family; he felt like an outsider. He was an outsider; they were used to getting along without him. Nobody interesting to talk to. There was the short respite during their customary drive to the West Country, the only place outside his ship where he feels at home. Martha didn't like it there, said it was too cold and barren and the food was awful. John was fretting because the tiny village shop didn't sell Disney comics. Meea was out and about with her cousin, Marit, which was fine. Neither of the children liked the dinners which mainly consisted of boiled salted fish, potatoes and carrots. They are both fussy eaters and thin and weedy. Martha is pandering to them, feeding them the few things they will eat. Everything has to be just so or they'll rather go hungry than eat it. When he was young he had to jolly well eat what was on the table or not eat at all.

They decided that Bjørn and Randi could borrow the car and drive to the West Country for a much needed break taking Anders and Marie with them. The poor boy was working himself to death. Huge sigh of relief when they finally drove off down the road. Two weeks without a screaming infant and a house full of chattering people! On the second day they were back. Little Rune had fallen ill with diarrhoea and vomiting. Best thing to get him home. Kristoffer understood that, but the thought of another month in the house before he was finally due to join his ship in Marseilles . . . .

Help came unexpectedly, as had sometimes happened in his life. One day, when Martha was out shopping and had taken the kids with her with the promise of ice cream, the telephone rang. It was his Head Office: Sorry to interrupt his holiday, but the captain who had taken over his whip whilst he was on leave was being invalided home with suspected cancer. Would Captain Hoddevik mind terribly taking over when Tank Empress arrived in Rotterdam in three days? Kristoffer said yes without a second thought.

When Martha and the kids got back he immediately told her, which was the worst strategy. Martha flew into a rage: Oh yes, that was typical, his bloody ship was more important than everything else. But she was used to it. Never was he there when she needed him. And here he had been for two months, lying about on the sofa, playing cards with himself. Had it ever occurred to him to take the kids off her hands for a few hours, and how much work had he actually done on Bjørn's house! And what about the decking on the upstairs balcony that needed replacing? But of course, the damn ship was more important, always had been. Off he went whether she'd just had a baby or was due to have one any day!

In the end she had calmed down and he had driven to Hønefoss and bought planks of wood and started on the decking, which of course he didn't manage to finish. He had to pack as well and Martha, having got used to the idea that he was leaving a month early, made a good-bye party for him, inviting Anders and Marie who would have come anyway once they caught wind of a party. The atmosphere was good. Martha always puts on a good spread. Only little Meea was quiet, clinging to his arm, not wanting him to leave. She was different from the rest of them; he sensed that, the only person interested in listening to his records and one day he had come across her sitting at his desk in the small, little used room they called the library, looking at the photos in his box. He hadn't said anything and when he next looked in on her she was reading what looked like a grown-up book. He'd wanted to ask her what she was reading but thought better of it. She'd obviously gone to the library to have some time to herself. Martha was trying to get her interested in housework but that was a lost cause, like him and farm work. He suspected that spending hours walking about with Rune in his pushchair was really about having a legitimate reason to stay out of the house.

Still, he shouldn't be too hard on Martha. She had grown up under softer and easier circumstances than his sisters. People in the East were simply made of less sturdy stuff, that was the long and short of it. Martha kept complaining that having two babies in relatively quick succession in her late 30s hadn't been easy, and now there was a grandchild as well. Not the easiest of infants to look after, often grizzly and always into things. Once he had somehow got to a bottle of bleach and poured it all over himself, ruining his clothes and the new lino they'd just had put down in the kitchen; thank God he hadn't tried to drink it. But what about his mother then, who'd had seven children, eight if you counted little Augusta who died, and still managed to do her farm work! Her hard life had taken its toll though. At forty she had looked like an old woman; whereas Martha, 46 years old, still had a good figure.

But here he is, on his favourite run, down the west coast of Africa. Following the strip of land in the distance past deserts and jungles and down along the foggy coast of German West Africa, the Skeleton Coast with whispering skeletons of long dead men scattered about and half buried in the sand, or so he imagined.

He loved this run, the freedom of it, sailing with the Albatross around the Cape of Good Hope. Forgetting about things back home, the injustice, the rotten labour government who had stolen the money that should rightfully have come to the sailors. And no recognition. The Norwegian war-sailors got more gratitude from the Brits than from their own government. Churchill had pronounced that the sailors of the Norwegian merchant fleet were worth more than a million soldiers. His transport minister, Philip Noel-Baker had said it even more clearly and these were his exact words: "The first great defeat for Hitler was the Battle of Britain. It was a turning point in history. If we had not had the Norwegian fleet of tankers on our side, we should not have had the aviation spirit to put our Hawker Hurricanes and Spitfires into the sky. Without the Norwegian merchant fleet, Britain and the Allies would have lost the war." Somewhere else he had read that 40% of the fuel had been transported on Norwegian tankers. But nobody in Norway said anything about this. And the Nortraship money was gone . . .

Sun still high in the sky. Tank Empress, his ship, the engine humming, ploughing through the glittering waves, incredibly smooth run this. Not always so, but this time they'd had nothing but good weather. Nobody had gone crazy. Nobody had been difficult or disruptive. No problem except for Ordinary Seaman Roar Hansen. He had signed on while Kristoffer was on leave, a short and unassuming man in his mid-forties, keeping himself to himself as far as Kristoffer had gathered. There was something wrong with his back, giving him a hump and he walked with a slight limp. One day as Kristoffer was sitting in his quarters writing his log there was a knock on the door, and in came Roar Hansen, uncertain, looking as if he wanted to flee, but instead summoned up his courage and handed Kristoffer a bottle, and in the bottle was a ship, a schooner. He had made it himself in his spare time, and now he wanted his captain to have it. Kristoffer looked at the schooner in the bottle. Not an easy thing to make and he had seen better ones. But Hansen had taken great care and even managed to paint blue waves on the inside of the bottle and underneath the ship. A totally unexpected gift. Kristoffer asked him in and offered him a glass of whisky and soda which Hansen gratefully accepted. Hansen didn't say much at first, but then the whisky loosened his tongue and he told Kristoffer that he really liked being on his ship, and that he came from a small place in the South Country and that all the men in his family had been sailors. He had been injured during the War. When his ship was torpedoed he'd been thrown across the deck and lost consciousness. As they abandoned ship he'd been left for dead, but then one of his mates had seen a slight movement and they'd got him into the lifeboat just before another torpedo split the ship in two. He'd been lying on the bottom of the lifeboat drifting in and out of consciousness for three days until they'd been picked up by a British corvette and he'd been taken to hospital in Belfast. Turned out his back was broken below the shoulder-blades and his pelvis fractured in two places. But he'd been really lucky, the break in his back had not moved, if it had, he would have been paralysed from the shoulders down. Yes, he'd been very lucky indeed, he'd recovered enough to keep working . . . No, he didn't have a family of his own, only a sister and an ageing mother. Kristoffer liked him, he was modest and genuine, looking straight at him with honest blue eyes—and the way he showed his appreciation, not many people thought of something like that. After the second whisky Kristoffer said that he could always come to his quarters for another chat. Normally he didn't fraternise with ordinary crew members but in this case he felt that it was the right thing to say. He didn't really think Hansen would take him up on it, but then again, you never know.

A few days went by. Hansen had not come back, and his bottled ship was gleaming on Kristoffer's desk. Then, one evening just as the sun was sinking into the sea, Tommy Svensen, another ordinary seaman, knocked on his door and told him that Roar Hansen had been found dead on the foredeck, a stroke or a heart attack, they thought, They had covered the body and now they were wondering what to do . . .

And there he is, lying in a box in the freezer-room. His mother and sister have been told. They want the body to come home so they can give him a proper burial next to his father.

Kristoffer can't get Roar Hansen out of his mind. Thinking of the poor man and his modest life—his happiness simply to be fit to work—makes it hard to focus on anything else. Less than a week since he was sitting opposite him in this office, right there, in that chair . . . Tomorrow he'll write his sister and mother a letter, telling them what an honest and hardworking and well-liked crew member he was.

He knows the rocky coast of South Africa. The awesome mountains in the distance, craggy and green with what looks like deep gorges and ravines. Cape Town with its flat table top mountain. He has never been up there, barely set foot in the town, only anchored briefly for supplies. Fresh meat, potatoes, and fruit—crates of lemons, oranges and apples, mainly apples—large red apples, they last a long time when kept cool, juicier and more delicious than any apple you get in Europe. The company has ordered him to keep stumm about Hansen's body. He died in international waters, no suspicious circumstances, nothing to do with the South Africans but you never knew what sort of bureaucracy they might come up with. Kristoffer thinks of the penguins on the shore and the enormous landmass with its monkeys and lions and elephants which he has never seen, only knows that they are there. The coast is treacherous with under-water cliffs that so easily can tear large rifts in the hull and you're sunk within the hour. Many a ship has gone aground over the years. The important thing is to keep well away from the coastline. These must be the waters where the Flying Dutchman disappeared, its ghost forever condemned to sail the southern seas. Kristoffer likes to believe that it is still out there, but he hopes never to see it, for anyone who sets eyes on it is doomed. But the sea is teaming with life, whales and dolphins and all sorts of fish. Once he's sure he saw a sea-cow, the ancient mariners used to think they were mermaids.

Evening approaching, sun sinking fast. Kristoffer has spent most of the day at his desk, lots of formalities when a crew member dies, on top of his ordinary admin work.

Around him the cold Atlantic. The warmer Indian Ocean only starts when he has rounded Cape Agulhas, the southernmost tip of Africa, but less famous as it is less dramatic and less treacherous. People live there, unbelievably enough. He has never set foot there, only seen it from afar. That's what he does—navigating the waterways of the world, skirting the continents, anchoring in out-of-the-way places and seldom stopping long enough to get a look-in. But sometimes he does, like Bombay and Karachi—he was there often in 1943-44. Teaming with people, dirt and filth. Old toothless women coming up to him, reaching out their hands saying "no father, no mother, no sister, no brother, baksheesh, Maharajah, baksheesh". Life is hard in the slums of India and people live short and miserable lives, the toothless old women were probably younger than Martha is now.

The wild coast of South Africa. View of the Indian Ocean.
I was there but the albatross was nowhere to be seen.

That's it. The Cape of Good Hope is coming up on the port side, time to go out and look for the albatross. Kristoffer grabs his binoculars and walks out onto the foredeck. Somebody has laid down a small wreath where Hansen died. Kristoffer stops briefly and makes the sign of the cross. Then he scours the sky with his binoculars before realising that today he doesn't need them, for there they are, two of them, gliding, dancing on the wind, floating through the air right overhead, dark against the burning sky. Not so high up today. When they are exactly above him he can see their white wings with the much darker edges, their long fearsome beaks. He rushes back to his quarters and gets out his camera, waits till one of the albatrosses is right above his head, and takes his picture. Hopefully it will come out right, and he'll send it to Meea. He walks up to the prow. Standing there, looking ahead, it feels as though he is flying across the waters, flying with the albatrosses, the freedom of it all, no nagging wife or screaming infant or house full of people, only him, the sea and the albatrosses. He remains on deck following the birds with his eyes as they glide and float in wide circles over the ship. Night falls quickly. The giant birds are swallowed up by the dark and the lighthouse on the Cape is sending out its beams of warning. He enters the Bridge. Starboard now and then along the coast to Cape Agulhas. Tomorrow they'll have reached the Indian Ocean and with luck the albatrosses will still be there.

Late
November 1959

On an overcast November's day in 1959 the oil tanker, Tank Empress, was slowly making her way up the Oslofjord. She was huge, some 24,000 tonnes, one of the biggest in the world when she was built in Malmö, Sweden, in 1950. On board were the Captain, Kristoffer Hoddevik, plus 41 men and one woman. Most of them Norwegian but with a sprinkling of other nationalities as well, most famously two middle aged men from the Yemen. Abdullah and Mohammed. Many of the men had sailed together for years. They had been through the Panama Canal and to Kwinana in Western Australia. They had sailed through the Suez Canal and around the Cape of Good Hope. They had endured the oppressive heat of the Persian Gulf, and the storms of the ice-cold Atlantic. And now they were here, sailing up the Oslofjord. There had been quite a lot of snow, but then the temperature had risen, melting most of it away, subsequently the temperature had fallen turning the slush and water to mirrors of ice. But the crew had seen none of this, all they saw were the cliffs, islets and forests surrounding the Oslofjord with patches of snow in between. A landscape devoid of colour, like sailing through an old black and white film.

Captain Kristoffer Hoddevik was a strict and fair man of 57, much loved by all who sailed under his command. He didn't interfere with their work as long as it was done to his satisfaction. "There is always more than one way of doing a thing," he used to say, "so why should I assume that my way is the best." Besides, with his sturdy frame and broad West Country features he inspired confidence. He did not suffer fools. If a colleague was too full of himself, Dad soon took him down a peg or two. If a crew member was too happy-go-lucky or didn't take his work seriously he soon found himself out of a job. Still, Dad always knew the difference between a young sailor who tried his best all-be-it not very successfully and a lazy slob who couldn't be bothered. He knew a little about a lot of things, like when crew members fell seriously ill in mid-ocean and were saved by my father's medical knowledge. Secure in his position and in his worth, he saw no need to demonstrate his authority by parading about looking important, or by wearing his uniform when at sea. He loved his ship and his crew. His work was his life, navigating the oceans, finally to anchor by some out-of-the-way oilfield. We, his family, saw little of him and when he did come home he soon grew bored and restless.

* * *

The giant ship made its way up through the Sound of Drøbak where the German cruiser, Blücher was sunk on April 9th 1940. She was spearheading a fleet of warships on their way to occupy Oslo and to capture the King, Haakon VII, and his family. Blücher got as far as the sound between the tiny town of Drøbak and the island fortress of Oscarsborg. Norway was neutral at the time and hoped to remain so and was therefore ill-equipped for a German attack. All they had at Oscarsborg was two 40 year-old canons and one torpedo battery on the mainland. However, they did the job and Blücher was set alight and sunk. Out of the 2,202 crew and troops around 830 died, some drowned and some burnt to death in the burning oil. The survivors came ashore either side of the fjord. The captain, Heinrich Woldag, survived the sinking but was killed eight days later in a plane crash.

Sinking the Blücher did not stop the German invasion of Oslo. The city was captured from the air later in the day, but it did give the King and his family time to escape.

Blücher is still there today, resting at the bottom of the fjord. For many years her tanks kept leaking oil that now and then came bubbling up to the surface.

There were no canons or torpedo battery stopping Tank Empress as she made her way through the sound heading for the tiny town of Fagerstrand where she was to discharge her cargo of oil. It was only to be an over-night stay. No chance for the Norwegian crew members to see their family and friends. Many of them were annoyed to be so close and yet so far. Abdullah and Mohammed, were particularly excited. They loved their captain. Abdullah had been sailing on various ships for years but somehow he'd got

156

stranded in Marseille and was doing the rounds of the ships in the harbour asking for work; hungry, threadbare and miserable in a long coat that barely hung together, green with age. My father took pity on him and as he happened to need an ordinary seaman he decided to give him a chance. Mohammed was there already and the two became inseparable. They had never been this far north before and thought that the black, forested shoreline looked awesome and foreboding. So this was their captain's land! So cold that being out on deck was torture and all you wanted was to get back inside. They had heard a rumour that the captain's family was coming to visit and had planned their work so they could be on deck and watch them when they arrived.

I'll remember that day for as long as I live. Finally and unbelievably Dad's ship was coming to Norway, and not to the West Country where most ships landed, but to Fagerstrand on Nesodden just down the Oslofjord.

We set out early in the morning, Mum, Bjørn, Randi, John and I. Anders and Marie looked after Rune. Mum and Bjørn in front, and Randi, John and I in the back. Bjørn was driving. I adored Randi because she was so tall and beautiful and could barely contain my excitement that she was with us on this incredible day. Bjørn had driven to Oslo many times, but Nesodden was unfamiliar territory.

What I remember best from Nesodden is driving through dense forest on gravel roads that seemed to go on for ever and lead nowhere. As in all such places the roads were intended for local peole who knew where they were going and didn't need road signs. Consequently the signposting left a lot to be desired. Finally we thought we had reached Fagerstrand but all we found was a desolate nowhere with a tiny wooden pier covered in ice, which was where the road ended. We had to turn round, but there was nowhere to turn except on the icy pier which was barely bigger than the car. Mum, Randi, John and I got out so that if the car slid and landed in the water Bjørn would be the only one soaked. We assumed he would get out and swim to the surface, but even so . . . Holding our breath we stood watching as he carefully manoeuvred the car around. When he was safely back on the gravel, nose pointing the right way, we got back in and our search for Fagerstrand continued.

We saw the ship before realising that we had finally arrived; a gigantic beast, long and elegant, like a living and breathing organism resting by the quayside. Tank Empress, large as life, anchored by a Norwegian forest of fir trees.

Fagerstrand wasn't much of a place, only a few houses and other buildings and some enormous oil tanks. We parked, collected our bits and pieces and walked up the gangway, steely grey water surging below us, cold and uninviting. And there, Dad on the gangway, in his uniform which I had never seen him wearing before, tall and strong, his sharp greyish-green eyes shaded by his uniform cap. So this was Tank Empress, the ship that I had heard so much about but never set eyes on, Dad's kingdom. He led us across the deck to his quarters which consisted of three fairly big rooms; a lounge and two bedrooms and a bathroom, as far as I remember. Everything like a normal flat, yet totally different. The windows were round for starters. The walls had dark mahogany panelling and a smell of distant lands and Dad's after-shave hung in the air. So this was where Dad lived when he was not with us!

Dad opened a bottle of champagne which I had heard about but never tasted. Being nearly 12 I was considered old enough to have a glass. It wasn't sweet like I had imagined, but rather bitter, and the bubbles were sharp, but having finally been thought old enough for a grown-up drink I wasn't going to let on that I would have preferred lemonade, like John.

We sat around and talked for a while. There was a box of foreign chocolates, sweet milk chocolates with a soft centre, my favourite. A while later the Chief Steward arrived, bowed and announced that dinner was served. It made me feel very special, like I had suddenly become part of a rich aristocratic family. We went downstairs where a long table with a white table cloth was laid for us. There were other people present as well; I think the First and Second Officer and the Chief, plus an attractive young woman, the Radio Operator, plus one or two others. There and then I decided that I too would become a Radio Operator and sail the world. The food was mouth-watering, some sort of clear broth with tiny button mushrooms and bright green peas. There were potatoes and salty meat and some large red apples, beautiful and delicious, nothing like the apples we had in Norway. Apart from this all I remember about the meal is that I loved it and that the Chief Steward was serving us dressed in a white jacket.

Later on Dad took me up to the Bridge and showed me the radar, a screen with a luminous needle going round and round and the surrounding islands showing up like luminous dots. We spoke English then. I had started learning English at school that autumn and Dad was amazed at how much I had picked up already. Our English teacher was a 38-year old Scottish woman, much more inspiring than old Mr Frohaug. And all the while I could hear the hum and heartbeat of the engine. A different world, separate from the islands and forests of south-eastern Norway.

Then there was the booze. People smuggled alcohol because the prices in Norway were ridiculously high and nobody saw it as doing anything wrong—more like an up yours to the government's ludicrously strict alcohol policy. A man from customs was sitting in a small room across the corridor. Bjørn and Dad had to go out and check that the car was parked all right, that was their story in case the customs man asked. They hid bottles under their coats and off they went. The customs man was staring at them pretending to read a magazine. A while later they had to go to the car again, something they had forgotten to bring inside. More bottles under their coats. Customs man staring and pretending to read, but he didn't stop them.

Next morning the Chief Steward came and announced that breakfast was served. Good fresh bread, delicious salami, salty sliced meat, some weird and wonderful cheese, the same delicious apples as the night before. Food from far-away places, familiar, yet different.

Our mood was not so buoyant now. Soon the ship would be sailing. We'd have to leave the exotic world of the ship, and the fairy-tale would be over. No telling when we would next see Dad. Somebody came and asked when exactly he wanted to sail. Dad was in his white vest, putting on his shirt in brusque, manly movements. He finished getting into his shirt whilst giving the order. 'Yes, nine o'clock sharp, that will do.' This epitomises my father, never taking himself too seriously, never worrying about appearances or if one of his crew members should see him without his shirt on.

My memories of the morning are hazier than of the previous day. I remember the episode with the shirt and Dad's command as taking place after breakfast, but it must have been before. Dad would not have gone down to breakfast in his vest. I remember what I was wearing; a pink jumper and a checked pleated skirt with the same shade of pink as the jumper. My hair was short then, although for most of my life I've had fairly long hair. I can't remember what kind of coat I had or what anyone else was wearing, except that Bjørn's coat was navy and the bottles he smuggled out had made him look portly.

Now I'm wondering; why did we drive off so promptly? Why didn't we remain on shore for a while to see the ship all lit up and slowly glide away from the quayside and sail off down the Oslofjord, cutting through the water, exhaust from her funnel, until she disappeared behind an island or a headland, or simply faded into the grey light of morning. It would never happen again, so why didn't any of the adults think to give us this memory to hold on to?

Our drive back to Oslo has gone from my memory, disappeared without a trace. What I do remember is that Mum, Randi, John and I took the bus from Oslo. The reason must have been that Bjørn had to go straight to work and would drive the car back in the evening. Neither Mum nor Randi could drive at the time. We sat on the bus for about an hour and outside the day was dank and flat and rainy. The bus wasn't cold, yet I felt a chill in my bones and tiredness behind my eyes, the way you feel after insufficient sleep in an unfamiliar bed. But most of all it was the disappointment of it all being over so soon. A bleak day stretching ahead—back to a cold and empty house. We'd been given the day off school but now I hoped we'd get back in time to catch the last couple of hours.

Many months later when Dad came home on leave he brought three red leather wallets, one for each of us. Abdullah had given them to him after we left. That was when he told Dad that he'd been hiding on deck to see us arrive. He had wanted to give us the wallets in person but felt too shy to do so. Such a pity. I would have given a lot to have met a man from the Yemen. The wallets were made of inferior leather and not very practical, but they were gifts from the heart and I treasured mine for years, keeping it safe in the chest of drawers in my room.

Tank Empress.

Liverpool, May 2013

You hear about a place, read about it, find out what it was like at a certain stage in history, impressions based on literature, photographs, films and hearsay, and when you finally get there—the feeling of recognition, of confirmation . . . you see what you expected to see, not exactly how you imagined it, but near enough.

As for harbour-side Liverpool I had only my imagination and impressions from novels to go by. I had pictured war-time sailors walking ashore to a maze of crooked and dingy streets of smoke-stained houses and shabby pubs needing only to walk a hundred metres to enter a waterhole where they could drown their traumas and heal their frazzled nerves in the arms of a woman. I had hoped that some of those pubs would still be standing, their interior more or less unchanged, walls and woodwork darkened by age and smoke from a time when people could smoke in pubs. I did see some old pubs further away and very likely they were there in the 40s. My point is that harbour-side Liverpool is nothing near the way I had imagined it.

I arrived in Liverpool in the company of my friend and colleague Chris. He had grown up in Liverpool and wanting to see some of the places that my father had visited, I asked his advice about how best to see the relevant areas. It turned out that Chris' father, Jim, is a historian specializing in local history and the Second World War and that he would be happy to help. Chris wanted to see his father anyway, as he was due for a knee replacement the following week, and so we set off to Liverpool where we met up with his father.

I liked Jim the moment I set eyes on him—an old-school gentleman with a whiff of eccentricity; smart light trousers, navy blazer, pale-blue shirt and a colourful tie. After a tasty meal in an enormous Chinese restaurant, the most authentic in Liverpool, according to Chris and Jim, we set off on a drive in the footsteps of my father.

Where I had imagined dingy streets and time-worn pubs there was a high wall separating the road from a seemingly eternal line of warehouses dating back to the 18-hundreds. And what warehouses they were! Massive, old red brick, several floors, hundreds of metres long, like gigantic building blocks. My father must have seen them and been impressed. On the opposite side of the road, higher up, I noticed a terrace of tiny houses for the poor. Surely my father must have seen those too. Jim said that one warehouse had been used for storing grain. A young boy had once fallen in and drowned, suffocated by the grain. Jim was a child during the war and told us about the bombings that he remembered very well, he had even experienced a near miss. On August 31st 1940 a single German plane had unloaded a string of bombs around the custom House and machine-gunned Castle Street and James Street, exactly where he and his father had passed less than an hour before.

We drove on. Jim telling us about his childhood, how his family had gone to live with his grandparents in the outskirts of Liverpool because it was safer, and how he had roamed the countryside on his bike, a freedom present-day children do not have, due to the low-life that prey on them.

We left the city behind and for a while we drove through what looked like countryside. Jim parked the car and said: 'This is where your father would have discharged his oil.' A totally peaceful and deserted spot. An unmade-up car park, gorse in bloom, an embankment, a band of green, a paved footpath along the Mersey, a metal fence. A couple of low brick buildings surrounded by pink fences, storage or pump houses . . . I don't know. I scrambled down the embankment and walked along the footpath where the Mersey was sloshing against the muddy shore in lazy grey waves. Further along the path an elderly man in a high visibility anorak was sitting on a bench, his fishing rod propped against the fence. No sign of an oil tank or a tanker anywhere.

Back in the car Jim stopped after about five minutes to show me where gigantic oil tanks had once stood. These days the grass-covered foundations are all that remain.

On the way back to Liverpool proper Jim told us the story of two ships the Malakand and the Mahout and the total destruction of the Malakand, as far as I gather Liverpool's worst explosion of the war. The Malakand and Mahout were in the Huskinsson dock on the evening of May 3rd 1941 with the greater part of the cargoes consisting of 500-lb. bombs, the Malakand loaded with over 3590 tons of these aboard. According to Jim the attack started at 10.30pm and a shower of incendiaries fell on the Malakand's No.1 hatch and not more than a few seconds later a semi-inflated balloon fouled the forestay and descended on to the hatch. There was an instantaneous sheet of fire, mast high. The hatch covers were ablaze. By 11pm, the crew had extinguished the fire with sand and the ship's hoses. But a few minutes after eleven the shed alongside received two direct hits from heavy bombs and immediately caught fire. Jets of fierce flames enveloped the Malakand and very soon she was burning. The crew stayed aboard until midnight, fighting a losing battle with flames sweeping from bow to stern and the explosive cargo growing hotter every minute. The vessel was eventually abandoned but the fight continued from the wharf. A mobile fire unit arrived at 1am, but it was difficult to get near the ship. At 7.30am the Malakand blew up. Plating and castings were found half a mile away, but miraculously the crew suffered no casualties, as they had worked the hoses to the bitter end. The Mahout escaped with only some damage.

Our next stop was Crosby Beach, a beauty-spot near my hotel, the Royal. We parked beside a yellow Rolls Royce with a lone young woman sitting by the wheel staring out to sea. Blond hair in a ponytail, yellow shirt under a blue jumper. Classic and expensive clothes but that doesn't explain the inimitable *je ne sais quoi* of wealth and class combined—the serene expression of someone who has never had to worry about bills and the price of food.

We had stopped by the beach to see the tankers as they sailed into harbour further along, and I did see one. I walked along the sandy shore—the open space, the air, the wind, the sea. The estuary opening up to the Irish Sea and further on to America. An Iron Man standing close by, knee-deep in water, further out two more Iron Men, one waist-deep and one with only his head showing. Antony Gormley's sculptures that I had heard about but never thought of seeing. Very fitting this—my father dubbed the Iron Man because of his capacity to stand on the bridge for three days and nights in a row, and now there are real iron men guarding the estuary towards the Irish Channel that he sailed all those years ago.

Peace, hardly any people about. Difficult to believe that this is the edge of a busy city. Why didn't more people come out here? Again and again I filled my lungs with the fresh air of the sea. The last time I walked along a sandy shore was nearly two years ago, on the Skeleton Coast of Namibia. Jim and Chris were standing by the car. Happy enough it seemed, father and son who get on well but don't see each other that often. Still, I felt bad about spending so long on the beach and asked Jim if he minded and he replied 'not at all'.

The yellow Rolls Royce with the young woman was no longer there.

I understood my father better. The sea had been his love. Sea, glittering, shining. The expanse, steely grey, nuances of blue, a wide endless space stretching ahead until sea meets sky in an ever distant line. The freedom. The engine humming. The ship cutting through the water. He knew the highways of the oceans, knew the winds and the fog. The sea ever changing, sometimes rough and angry, sometimes glittering like silver. He loved it all.

I was struck by the mediocrity of my life in London. Off to work in the morning, walking through the park, the highlight of my day, a cappuccino from the nice lady at the station. Work, teaching, explaining grammar, marking, discussing work-issues with colleagues, keeping up a persona that isn't me. Journey home in the rush hour, crowds everywhere. Back in the house, cooking dinner. After dinner, TV. A glass or two of wine to take the edge off the boredom. The life of thousands of women throughout the UK. Not bad, just limited by circumstance and the lack of courage to break free. Or worse; the life of an elderly woman with an ailing husband; his deep-seated fear of imminent death permeating everything and stopping him from living. And the woman—having to use all her strength not to be sucked into the wake.

The sea, the space, the air. I could stay here for ever.

This is what my father had. The war was horrific but it was only five years out of a lifetime. When he was invalided home from the sea at the age of 60 it was as though his real life was finished. He never developed much enthusiasm for anything else.

Eventually I managed to tear myself away from the sea and join Jim and Chris. Jim took us back to his flat for tea. Turned out he had collected a lot of information about the blitz on Liverpool and the Battle of the Atlantic.

And amazingly, he had managed to find the article about the explosion on the Herbrand on the Internet and made up two photos of my father. A lovely and genuine man, my father would have liked him.

After tea he drove me back to the hotel. My plan was to write down my impressions but no way could I remain indoors with that wonderful shoreline just round the corner, and tomorrow I'd be back in the noise and pollution of London. So, I made my way across the marshland to the shore I had visited earlier. The tide had gone out and there were sand flats where there had been deep water a couple of hours ago. The iron men that had been knee-and chest-deep in water were on dry land with seaweed and barnacles clinging to their bodies. Further out and all around stood men that had been totally submerged until a while ago. No big ships were coming in or out. They can only sail at high tide.

One of Antony Gormley's iron men staring out across The Irish Sea

The following morning I took the bus to the Albert Dock where the Maritime Museum is situated. A large section was dedicated to the Battle of the Atlantic. Paintings and photos of stricken ships belching smoke and Liverpool in flames and German planes dropping bombs. Long and informative texts with each picture. Mannequins in authentic uniforms. Model interiors of ships to show the sailors' living conditions. A running film of enormous waves sloshing over the deck of a ship gave you the feeling of what it must have been like out there, on the Atlantic, in a winter's storm. Room upon room of exhibits and illustrations. But, it was all about the British sailors and the British navy, merchant and military, not a word about the Norwegian sailors without whom the British would not have won the war. Nothing about the 3,628 Norwegian sailors who lost their lives during the Battle, and the many more who had to live out their lives with physical and psychological disabilities. You may say that in the context of the war 3,628 individuals is a fairly insignificant number. But not so insignificant when you consider that in 1940 the whole population of Norway counted fewer than three million. Still, this is a British museum and it is reasonable that history should be represented from a British point of view. I understood this and decided that it would be interesting to visit the Maritime Museum in Oslo to see the Battle described from a Norwegian point of view, because there would surely be a lot about the war over there too.

After a walk around the harbour area I took the bus back to the hotel where I had left my overnight bag.

Sitting on the bus I contemplated the long terraces of time-worn little houses, wondering whether my father had once ventured down those very streets. The bus stopped and an ancient woman dressed in beige—almost bent double, white hair with a yellow rinse—struggled onto the bus with her shopping trolley. And I thought: You were alive back then, a young woman you must have been. You might even have seen my father in the street. Weird to think that what is ancient history to me is still real and alive to people who were actually there. The past not so dead and long gone at all.

Greenock, February 25th 2014

I'm sitting on a Virgin train flying through the English countryside on my way to Greenock for a rendezvous with my father.

You don't understand a nation or its people until you have seen some of the country.

In Norway the landscape is constantly changing. Deep dark coniferous forests, undulating farmland, idyllic lakes, mountains of rock and eternal snow and valleys—each with its unique dialect and architecture. If you are in the Oslo area and want to make your way west, you start in the low-land among farms and lakes. After a while the landscape changes, trees grow smaller. Soon there are no real trees, only tiny mountain birches, bent and twisted from the weight of icy winds and snow. Climb higher and you are on a plateau where only mosses, lichen and heather can grow. Higher still and you're in a stone desert, eternal snow all around.

Dramatically changing seasons. Deep snow in winter. Cold. The blue light of daybreak and dusk. Violent spring, everything wakes up and returns to life in the space of a few weeks. By early June Norway has caught up with England. In the south sunshine till 10—11pm, midnight-sun in the north. Lovely and warm, wildflowers everywhere. Autumn, vivid colours—red, orange, yellow—stronger than in England. November, trees without leaves, everything grey and black, a landscape devoid of colour, and finally snow starts to fall, silent and pure.

The train has reached Wigan and the landscape is still unchanged, flat and monotonous. Same old-looking houses, 1880s perhaps. A factory with a tall chimney. I have no idea where Wigan is, should have brought a map of Britain. Landscape perhaps slightly more hilly. What looks like a low mountain range to the right, but mainly fields, copses, small forests, here and there a farm or a minor town. Just passing through what looks like a new town with rows of 1970-80s style houses.

Pleasant and gentle countryside, pleasant and gentle people, their conversation neutral, unthreatening, masters of small-talk "keep your opinion to yourself". Norwegians take the opposite approach, speaking their mind, sometimes embarrassing a stranger with direct and personal questions.

We're in Preston. Finally worked out how to use the map on my mobile. Lifelong habit this—having to know exactly where on the globe I happen to find myself. Preston is east and slightly south of Blackpool. Climbing towards the Lake District. At last some different scenery. Passing through the Lake District. Can't see any lakes. Mountains, or hills by Norwegian standards, bare and green. Pity I can't smell the air. We stop at a station. The 50-something woman on the opposite side of the isle stands up, wraps a thick scarf round her neck, puts on an anorak, she's wearing heavy walking boots, and leaves. A quick breath of air from a colder and wilder world as she opens the door.

Carlisle. Fortress-like structure to my right. Huge stone wall. I know nothing about Carlisle.

The Lake District. I've been there only twice in my 40 years in London. During our first or second summer in Britain we joined the Egyptian students on an overnight trip to Manchester and the Lake District. The majority were male PhD students in their 30s and their wives. We slept in a student hostel somewhere in Manchester, and Maher and I and two young Egyptians spent the evening in a pub—a hazy memory of a murky room with middle aged people quietly drinking. Egyptians tend to have little interest in exploring the sites and atmosphere of a place. Consequently most of the group remained in the hostel cooking dinner and preparing packed lunches for tomorrow. The following day, which was a Sunday, we continued to Lake Windermere. I had heard about the Lake District but didn't think a lot of it once I was there—pretty enough, but not on the same scale as the Norwegian mountains. The day was cold and blustery, which didn't help. I have a vague memory of a short walk along the lake and eating fish and chips in an old fashioned café with a waitress in black and white, but that's all.

Our second visit was by car during the Easter break of 1994—my first year in my university position, which is why I remember which year. Maher, Sam and I drove up to Manchester to visit Phyllis, a scientist that Maher had met on a conference in Japan, and who hovered on the periphery of our lives for a few years. Somewhere along the way we took a wrong turn and ended up driving across the Pennines from Sheffield. Suddenly we were in a different world, a narrow road, not much vegetation. Wild and desolate, hardly any traffic. An awesome cold grey lake, water sloshing against a stony shore. And it had started to snow, great big snowflakes fluttering through the air. It could have been Norway. Saturday afternoon. We passed a family out on a walk. Youngish mother and father, two children. All red cheeks, colourful anoraks and muddy boots. We slowed down as we drove past them. The scene made an impression because it was so sudden and unexpected.

On the Sunday Phyllis drove us to the Lake District because Sam and I wanted to go there. Again we stopped at Lake Windermere, which I did recognise from 15 years ago. The weather was sunny and pleasant and Sam and I were looking forward to a nice fresh walk. We had lunch. But then Phyllis dragged us to a shop where she spent ages looking at hand-knitted sweaters with dogs and sheep. There was still snow higher up. Sam was only 13 and wanted to touch it and so did I. Finally we set off past picturesque white houses with gardens full of daffodils and amaryllises in the windows. Maher didn't say anything but it was clear he would sooner have sat in a café drinking coffee, or headed back to Manchester. Phyllis' elegant boots were bothering her. Eventually we were within 50 yards of the snow. Phyllis was exhausted and sat down by the roadside. Maher said to Sam and me: "Right, that's enough." The poor boy couldn't believe that we were turning back so close to the snow. I understood better. Phyllis had been kind to invite us and to drive us all the way to the Lake District, and if her boots were hurting her feet . . . Sam took it well, although he never forgot it. We hadn't come to the Lake District to hang around indoors. Love of fresh air and open spaces versus a taste for cafés and shops. So we trundled back to the car and back to Manchester where Phyllis had a half prepared meal ready and waiting.

Enough about our journeys past. As I left the train in Greenock, the rain was pouring from a cold and unfriendly sky. I scurried into the nearest shelter, a messy old fashioned shop selling baby-clothes with a friendly blond woman behind the counter. I asked where I could find a taxi and she replied "round the corner" taking me to the door and showing me which particular corner she was referring to.

I am sitting in my hotel room in Greenock. Arrived here yesterday. In front of me is my father's little black diary from 1945. It has been to Greenock before. For one night, between February 22nd and 23rd, he stayed at the Adelphi Hotel. My hotel is quite old. It is not called the Adelphi. There is no hotel in Greenock, as far as I have been able to establish, with that name. Still, it might be the same one. Hotels keep going for years. Name, ownership and décor may change and facilities improve, but the purpose of the building remains the same. I really would not be surprised if this hotel was once called the Adelphi. It is central and of a good standard. The sort of place that would be recommended to a tired captain wanting a peaceful room for the night. I'm happy here. Earlier today I took a taxi to Great Harbour where the Herbrand was once anchored. Still a large harbour area on the outskirts of town, modern ships, not very busy, not many people about, calm grey water, cool fresh air. The taxi driver pointed to a ferry or cruise liner and said that this was the place where the ships used to dock during the war. My father was there, walked down the gangway and took a taxi into town, most likely wearing a suit, hat and overcoat—the gentleman's get-up of the day. But somehow I cannot picture it. The harbour area looks too modern. The feel of the past is gone.

Other vistas remain the same: Long terraces of council estates up in the hills. I asked the driver how old? He replied that they were built in the 1930s, so my father must have seen them, as he must have seen the large church or perhaps cathedral near the railway station which he must have used when travelling to London. It looks old. Modern ticket office, but the red brick work is worn and crumbling.

Weird weather, rain and sunshine constantly alternating. One minute the hills on the opposite side of the fjord disappear in a cloud of rain. The following minute they appear clear as day, snow on the distant mountain tops. Not unlike western Norway. My father must have felt at home, a good place to sit out the remainder of the war. Never in my life have I seen so many magnificent rainbows in one day. Torrential rain; got drenched in spite of my umbrella.

So these are the streets my father once walked on his way to and from the doctor—the dentist—the Nortraship office. The town has a slightly down-beat atmosphere, people looking care-worn and threadbare. It used to be an important industrial and shipping town, but has been in decline since the 1970s with a falling population. I walked through a large shopping centre where most of the shops belonged to the lower end of the market. Returned to the hotel, spent a couple of hours drying out in my room.

Another walk through town. A lot of handsome stone buildings that must have been built long before 1945. I continue up into the hills—greenery, gorse in bloom, peaceful streets with modern up-market houses most likely from after the war. The streets are empty except for the odd car or young mother pushing a buggy. The air is so cool and pure you could drink it. My father is unlikely to have ventured up here though. A keen walker he was not. Right now the sun is shining and a rainbow so clear that it looks almost solid has appeared above the hill, but the sunshine won't last. Black clouds are gathering across the Clyde telling me to make a hasty retreat, or else! I imagined I'd be enjoying the peace and open landscape, but gorse or no gorse, rainbow or no rainbow—the whole place has a desolate feel that makes me want to return to my room, reading and writing my journal. Then again, visiting a place on your own, on a rainy day, can make the most solitary person feel lonely. Or perhaps it's the emptiness one feels when stepping away from the trivia and trappings of one's life.

I'm taking all my meals in the hotel. The bar/dining room is warm and friendly. An old fireplace. No live fire, only an artificial tree covered in tiny electric light-bulbs in the grate, the sort of thing that looks tacky in a home but here it brightens the room and makes it look cosy and festive. The dinner is good; pan-fried salmon, fresh and firm, not like the several days-old farmed stuff you get in London; with vegetables and two glasses of wine, ice cream with raspberries for desert. Quite a few people . . . two elderly ladies with dyed blond hair, a group of burly Scots at the bar, another lone woman, what I assume to be a family of four—aging parents with their middle aged children—locals out for a meal most likely. Not a bad night at all. And tomorrow I'm going back to London.

The changing weather of western Scotland. Patch of sunshine in the distance.

"What War-sailors?"

The bus arrived in Oslo soon after 10am. I walked through the tiny park with its vibrant flower displays, sculptures and fountains and past the block-like brick structure of the City Hall, in its time controversial for looking more like a giant ware-house than a city hall, but magnificent inside, the walls decorated with paintings from Norse mythology. From there I made my way across an open space criss-crossed by tram lines and on to the harbour and the pier of boat 91 to Bygdøy. The whole walk took me just over ten minutes.

A lot of things have changed in Oslo—it's become more modern, more cosmopolitan, but the harbour area has stayed the same, reminiscent of the small provincial city it once was and still is compared to a metropolis like London. Tall structures of concrete and glass, not unlike Canary Warf, and a shiny opera house of white marble have sprung up, whilst other things remain safe and familiar, like a well-worn shoe. The little boats to Nesodden, Bygdøy and the other islands in the Oslo Fjord anchor where they have always anchored, and you can still buy freshly cooked prawns from modest booths by the waterside, if you know where to find them. And, on the cliff above towers Akershus Castle as it has done for the past 700 years. My father would have recognised it all.

Bygdøy is a peninsula that houses not only the Viking Museum, the Folk Museum, the Fram Museum and the Kontiki Museum but also the Maritime Museum. In addition it is one of the most prestigious addresses in Norway and the huge white villas with their shining black roof tiles and lush gardens are a joy to behold. I had taken the boat to Bygdøy and visited the museums on several occasions, but never the Maritime Museum.

The pier was almost deserted when I arrived. A look at the timetable told me that there was a boat every half hour and that I had arrived right in between. A few people were hanging about waiting for the next boat due to depart at 10.45. I walked around and took a couple of photos of the Castle and an enormous gull perching right in front of me. A Chinese or Japanese girl handed me her camera asking me to take a picture of her. A man of around 50 dressed in a brown cord jacket and a long purple scarf was marching up and down, speaking French into his mobile. He had the indefinable *je ne sais quoi* that's so hard to achieve unless you're born with it. Norwegians rarely have it. Few British people have it except for archetypal aristocrats and academics that mainly exist in books.

The boat arrived and the twelve or so people who had been gathering got on. Low season, so plenty of room. I found a window seat facing the direction of the boat. The Frenchman sat down opposite me but worked out that he was facing the wrong way and found a different seat, or perhaps he felt that he was invading my space.

The Maritime Museum is housed in a modern brick building on the waterfront. It's spacious and not at all unfriendly. I walked up to the young man at the reception desk and said I was only interested in the war-sailors and where could I find the section dedicated to them? The young man looked blank. 'The war-sailors? No, no there is nothing about the them here. There used to be a couple of pictures over there', he nodded towards the cafeteria, 'but they had to be removed to make room for the exhibition of the paintings of Karl Erik Harr'. Harr is a Norwegian artist born in 1940 and known for his seascapes and boat paintings. I could understand that the Maritime Museum would be the ideal place for his exhibition, but what about the war-sailors? The young man thought that next year they might put on some kind of exhibition about them.

I entered the cafeteria and found the walls covered in Harr's paintings and drawings. Vivid and dramatic works mainly depicting sailboats and stormy seas. Not one picture of burning tankers and exploding ammunition ships, that I could see.

I was shocked. I knew there would be nothing like what I had seen in Liverpool, about the Battle of the Atlantic. But that there was absolutely nothing at all about the war-sailors! No, that was too hard to comprehend.

All those men, and women, who had died or risked their lives—gone and forgotten, no attempt to keep their memory alive! It beggared belief.

The receptionist told me that I would probably find some information in the library upstairs and by the way, the library was free and I could sit in the reading room as long as I liked.

The librarian, a young blond man in his mid-20s, was helpful, possibly because his services were not exactly in high demand. I seemed to be the only visitor. He brought me three heavy folders each containing several annuals of *Krigsseileren*, (The War-sailor). Leafing through the magazines I found what I was looking for: Articles about "war hazard pay"; the moneys that had been put into a special fund for the Norwegian sailors, and which they had been promised would be paid out to them after the war but of which they received not a penny. In 1972, after a long and bitter struggle, the Norwegian Parliament finally decided to pay an ex gratia sum of NOK 180 per month of active service to surviving seamen or their surviving relatives. The term ex gratia indicates that the Norwegian government felt under no obligation to pay the sailors at all, and the money, it was later discovered, did not come from the Nortraship Fund. 180 Norwegian Kroner is about £18 in today's currency. Obviously the relative value was higher in 1972 but it is still a negligible sum compared to what the sailors would have received had they been paid their due directly after the war as they had been led to believe. Even 180 Kroner would have been something back then. By 1972 much of the value had been eaten up by inflation.

Leafing through various issues of *Krigsseileren* I found a lot of articles and readers' letters about this treachery. For example, in 1983 one ex war-sailor, who was badly disabled from war injuries, was wondering how come the government would not pay out NOK 120 million to the war-sailors, but had no problem allocating NOK 150 million to a hospital in India which, to his knowledge, the Indians had not asked for.

In a different issue, also from 1983, I came across the following passage:

One day in the early summer of 1945—with all of Norway euphorically celebrating the end of the war—two men are taking a stroll along Oslo's harbour area. The two are Medical Student Odd Øyen and Captain Reidar Myhre, both prominent members of the resistance. Captain Myhre points towards some dismal workmen's huts where people live in appalling conditions. He says: 'Can you see the people living in those shacks? They are sailors who have made their way home to Norway, the maritime nation, after serving their country under hard and inhumane circumstances at sea . . . '

This episode must have made a lasting impression on Odd Øyen, for in the years that followed he became a determined spokesman for the war-sailors.

Years later it transpired that part of the fund had already been used up during the war to finance the Norwegian government in exile. The rest, it has since come to light, was used to rebuild the country after the devastation of the German occupation and Allied bombing. Apparently the long serving labour government, led by Einar Gerhardsen, helped itself to the fund to finance the establishment of the Norwegian Welfare State. In short, the much admired Norwegian social democracy achieved its claim to fame by embezzling money that should rightfully have gone to the war-sailors. This is still a controversial issue in Norway.

All in all the articles didn't tell me much that I didn't know already, and I soon felt that I had read enough so I went downstairs to the cafeteria for a sandwich and a coffee. In front of me at the counter was a group of 60-something American men and women who were clearly doing the rounds of the Bygdøy museums. They moaned a lot about the price of a cup of coffee and were surprised when the cashier refused to accept dollars. Perhaps they were from one of the cruise ships that dock below the Castle with only a few hours in Oslo. The cashier threw me a glance and shrugged. I liked him, an elderly man with an amiable face, a retired sailor most likely. When it was my turn I said to him:

'I came here to see what you've got about the war-sailors, and I'm seriously surprised that there is nothing, nothing whatsoever.'

'Don't be surprised,' he replied, 'ignoring the war-sailors has been a favourite Norwegian pass-time for years.'

Back outside. 20 minutes until the next boat. The sun was out. Soft green lawns, sparrows darting about. Nobody around except for a handful of people waiting by the pier. Wavelets lapping against the shore. White cumulus clouds above Oslo. And up in the hills overlooking the city resembling a medieval fortress—the old Sea Academy where my father was once a student, graduating with top marks in every discipline, the best student till that time; and possibly to date. You can't do better than top marks in every subject. He put some of his success down to using his common sense rather than quoting from books. It is no longer a Sea Academy. For a while it was a commercial college and now plans are afoot to turn it into a prestigious school of further education, the English equivalent to a 6th form college. The structure remains the same. The building is listed so they cannot tear it down or alter its construction. There is a clause that it must always be used for education.

I like old buildings; they are a link to the past, make it closer, more real. In Florence I saw the palace where Leonardo da Vinci painted the Mona Lisa. And there, on the other side of the narrow fjord is the building where my father walked the corridors, sat in the classrooms, looked out through the very same windows that are now reflecting the afternoon sun—contemplating the Oslo fjord—Bygdøy, Nesodden, the islands and shore line behind—dreaming about the future, a future that came and was gone in a flash; and in many ways did not work out as he had hoped. Such is life, here today, gone tomorrow, and many of the things that happen to us are outside our control.

* * *

In 1960 my father was awarded the *Norwegian Shipowner Association's gold medal* for faithfully serving his shipping company; *Sigurd Herlofsen & Co A/S* for 25 years. This was appreciated, but recognition of his valiant war contribution it was not.

* * *

Kristoffer Martin Elias Hoddevik passed away on January 13th 1983. In 1985 he was posthumously awarded the Defence Medal for services to his country.

The Defence Medal was established in 1945 as a reward for military and civilian personnel who participated against the German occupation of Norway as well as others who had demonstrated a solid national stance during the war. The presenting of the medal was discontinued during the 1950s. It was resumed in 1979; mainly for the benefit of the sailors who had served in the Merchant Navy during the war and had not received the recognition they deserved. The medal is still being awarded. No ceremony, just a medal in the post.

September
23rd 2013

6pm. Monday evening. I'm standing by the bus stop in Sundvollen on the very spot where all those years ago my father and King would wait for me as I arrived from Oslo where I lived. Home for a weekend or just for the afternoon, whenever I felt the need to get out of Oslo and back to the fresh air and tranquillity of my home. John is supposed to meet me but so far he hasn't turned up.

Many things are like before but some are different. The road is where it has always been, and so is the stream, down to a trickle now after a dry summer. Where there used to be long autumnal grass there is a car park. Only one corner has not been tarmacked over and the grass left to grow. The surrounding houses are still there and so is the little supermarket, now belonging to a chain not yet thought of back then. A couple of unattractive concrete buildings have sprung up—part of the hotel. There has been an inn here since the Middle Ages, originally for pilgrims on their way to St Olav's Shrine in Trondheim, or Nidaros as it was called then. In the 19th century the inn was expanded and turned into a hotel. It is now an up-market complex specialising in conferences.

The Old Man and King are gone.

In July 2011 images of the Sundvollen Hotel were flashed all over the world. It is the nearest hotel to Utøya and the atrocity that that took place on July 22nd. The hotel was nearly empty that Friday. My sister-in-law, Anne Cathrine, who is the chief receptionist, arrived for her shift anticipating an uneventful afternoon. It turned out to be anything but. Suddenly the hotel filled up with survivors from the atrocity. Their families trickled in, and the press of course. The management provided free food, rooms to sleep in and dry clothing, many of the youngsters had stripped down to their underwear before swimming for their lives across the cold lake. A hotel guest who happened to be a nurse had her hands full and worked tirelessly into the night. There were a lot of local heroes that day, neighbouring men and women who took to their boats to pick frozen and terrified kids from the water whilst being shot at from the Utøya shore.

The last time my father and King were waiting at the bus-stop on my account was on an August afternoon in 1973; the 15th to be precise. I remember the date because on the 16th I moved to England for good. Maher was in Norway with a one year scholarship from the Norwegian state. The Norwegian authorities took a tough stance on immigrants from third world countries and one of their biggest fears was that scholarship students would want to settle. Maher had tried to extend his visa, but had been refused and had to leave Norway the minute his year was up. By then we had been seeing each other for ten months and so agreed to make a go of life together in England.

What was I thinking? Nothing, except that I couldn't bear staying behind in Norway after Maher had left. Mum and Dad, on the threshold of old age, were hurt, devastated, disappointed. 'Nothing good will come of it', they said. I wanted to prove them wrong and packed my clothes and my most valued belongings into two suitcases. The things I didn't find room for—my walking boots, most of my books and my few kitchen utensils, I stuffed into a cardboard box which I put on the bus to Sundvollen where Dad had promised to collect it. You could send things by bus in those days, provided you paid and someone picked them up at the destination. The bus from Oslo arrived in Sundvollen at 25 minutes past every hour and I had asked Dad to be there at 4.25, or it might have been 5.25, but no later. Good old Dad . . . Earlier that summer he and Auntie Astrid had been to Canada. Several of their relatives and other people from back home had settled in Saskatchewan so there was no shortage of people who wanted to entertain them. My father was over 70, and his thoughtless relations had dragged, him—an elderly man who had been retired for years and had grown used to a regular routine and the silence of the Norwegian forests, from party to party until he got totally exhausted. On two occasions Auntie Astrid had been so worried about him that she looked in on him at night to check that he was breathing. After he got home, he was diagnosed with heart failure.

All that was happening on the periphery of my life. The only thing I could think of was going away with Maher and the exciting life I'd finally be leading , visiting the Orient, seeing the world.

I can picture my father now, standing at the bus-stop, the first chill of autumn in the air. Checked shirt, grey well-worn trousers, black beret glued to his head, King by his side, eager for the bus to arrive and me to appear. It must have been hard for Dad, waiting for the bus as he had done so often, but knowing that I would not be on it, only a cardboard box with my belongings, irrefutable evidence that I was going, leaving them for good. King would remain waiting, hoping that somehow I would appear from around the corner. And perhaps Dad would hope so too.

Asking Dad to drive to the bus stop and collect a box with my odds and ends was cruel. But Dad took it and forgave. Deep down I must have imagined the scene, but I preferred not to dwell on it as I was selfish, thinking only of the adventures ahead, and of Maher whom I imagined that I could not live without. Later, when I was lonely and the adventure had turned sour and we were poor and lived in a small flat with two young children whom I loved more than anything, but felt trapped and unhappy all the same, I believed that I had got what I deserved for abandoning my ageing parents.

Now I'm wondering, why did I ask Dad to collect the stuff? Why did I not simply give it away or leave it behind for whoever to make use of?

I have often thought of the times when our lives hang in the balance and the scales can tip this way or that and the outcome, whatever it is, is final and irrevocable. For me the afternoon of August 15th 1973 was one such time.

My last day in Oslo. The sun beating down. I have been spending the day packing and getting ready, and now I'm waiting at the bus-stop with my cardboard box. I feel tired and there is a dull ache behind my eyes—the sort of tiredness that only a good night's sleep can cure. But a good night's sleep is not on the agenda. Tonight Maher and I are having goodbye drinks with friends and tomorrow morning we'll have to get up at 4 to catch our plane to London. Why can't I just get on the bus, have a swim in the cool clean lake, King swimming next to me, pushing me gently with his front paw to make me turn round when he thinks I've swum too far out. After that supper with Mum and Dad and finally lie down in my childhood bed and sleep until I wake up by myself, as I have done so many times before.

The familiar red and yellow bus arrives. I lumber on with my box: 'How much to take this to Sundvollen?' A quick glance around the bus, the usual faces. And there's my cousin Rolf and his wife, Annie! They wave and point to an empty seat in front of them: 'Going home, are you?'

'Eh . . . yes, no . . . ' The bus is drawing me in, urging me to sit down. Yellow afternoon sun slanting through the windows, some passengers reading, others looking tired and sleepy. The driver is getting impatient: 'You don't need to pay for the box if you're going yourself.'

'No, no I'm not going.' I hand him the money and hurry back out. The red and yellow bus continues up the street, turns a corner, and is gone. I remember it clearly—the feeling that I was making a huge mistake and should have been on it.

At 6am the following morning Maher and I bordered an old propeller plane bound for London. Two and a half hours later we landed at Gatwick and my life had changed forever.

I disliked London from the start—too busy, too large, too grey, too heavy, too noisy, too complicated to find your way both literally or metaphorically. The seemingly infinite choices and opportunities were overwhelming and paralyzing. Eventually I did claw my way up to a decent position and to live in pleasant all-be-it not very exciting suburbs. There is of course Regents Park, Hampstead Heath and Islington Green; walks along the Thames and Regent's Canal . . . Still, the truth remains: London has never been a place of my heart.

And here I am again, September 2013, the same old bus-stop. John still hasn't turned up. I look around, and there, in the long yellow grass I see them—my father, his grey and green checked shirt, black beret on his head, looking smaller than I remember him. King at his side, pale-golden, nearly white, straining at his lead, happy to see me, and behind them—the black Austin Cambridge. I walk towards them, but then they are gone, vanished as if they were never there in the first place, the long yellow grass wafting slowly as if somebody has just walked through it and disappeared round a corner.

Part of me did remain on the bus that day, and there I still am, living in the house at the edge of the forest. Mum preparing a simple supper, and the four of us, Mum, Dad, John and I sitting down at the kitchen table. King at our feet, hoping for a treat.

I often wonder how my life would have turned out if I had got on the bus that day. I like to believe that I would have had an unusual but somewhat lonely existence guiding hikers around the deep forests telling them about history and the animals that live there. There is a lot to talk about; St Olav grew up in the area. In the early 17-hundreds there were battles between Norwegians and Swedish soldiers. Asbjørnsen and Moe, Norway's answer to the Grimm brothers, wandered through the forests collecting folktales from the locals. I would be writing and publishing books on myths and wildlife, and gradually becoming a legend in my own right.

The reality might have been less enthralling. With my parents growing older and Bjørn dying, leaving four sons aged 6 to 19 I could easily have been sucked into the role of family carer, especially if I had been single at the time of Bjørn's passing. My help and support would have been sorely needed. Randi worked hard as a waitress at the hotel in Sundvollen. My parents fed and looked after the younger boys when they got back from school. I would have had some teaching job or other, but my life would have been limited by family commitments, which although appreciated might well have been taken for granted. I might have turned into a bitter old maid, regretting not grabbing my chance when it was offered.

Not everybody comes to life-changing crossroads. Lots of people live their lives around the place where they were born. I've heard people saying: "I was born here, I've always lived here, and this is where I want to stay." There are choices of course: what kind of local job to take, which local girl to marry, what sort of house to live in, where to go on holiday . . . But nothing that totally changes the direction of their lives.

My father made bigger choices. There was no life for him in the village where he was born. With his sharp and crystal-clear mind he would have made an excellent lawyer. He could have worked his way through law-school. Or, he could have gone into partnership with Mr Laszinsky and set up home in Trinidad. Instead he chose to stay the course and return to a wife and son who had become unreal and distant. And I, I could have got on the bus that day in 1973 and my life and the lives of my family, and even Maher's life would have turned out differently.

In the end we do what our natures dictate us to do. My father loved the sea above all else, and it was not in his nature to be a quitter. In the same way, it was not in my nature to opt for an ordinary life in the familiarity and safety of home.

Still no John, perhaps he has forgotten. I could ring him, but it's OK. It's a lovely day, trees ablaze with colours. I might as well start walking.

* * *

The September dark is gathering outside the windows. We're all here, in the house that my father built in 1948. For a while we were sitting on the veranda, the forest whispering and breathing in the advancing dark, the liquid air of autumn growing colder, finally driving us inside. We were contemplating the northern sky that had turned bright green. The Aurora Borealis is less dramatic than further north. All we get is a faint echo of it from time to time, like tonight. We are different generations. None of us even thought of when my father sat on his ship in some distant harbour, designing the house he wanted to build if he ever made it back alive. But we who came after him are here: John, with his wife Åse. Bjørn's sons: Kai, Jarle and André, with their wives: Liv, Anne Cathrine and Vibeke, plus Kai's son, Kjetil. Bjørn's older son, Rune, passed away in 2004 aged 48. Anne-Lise is here too. To me this is the place of my heart, the landscape I first set eyes on as a child—the house I grew up in, always knowing that it was special. I rejected it as a young woman, not because I didn't love it, but because out there, in the wider world, there were fascinating people to meet and adventures to be had. These days I only return from time to time as a visitor, but at least there is that.

John and Åse have conquered their phobia of arranging a party for fear that they can't match the extravagant displays laid on by Kai and Jarle. I told them innumerable times: "People don't come here for the food. They come for the pleasure of simply being here, because the house contains some of their best childhood memories". So now, once in a while, they make a party serving soup, home-baked bread, cheese, wine and cake. Åse's fish soup is legendary, so thick it is more like a stew; with tomato, chilly and red peppers. She is quite an artist, and she collects beautiful glass and candles. Her glass purchases are everywhere, candlesticks, bowls, vases . . . The house is still my house, my home, nothing fundamental has been changed. The staircase is the same, the steps squeak where they have always squeeked. The banister, the two windows above the stairs, east-facing, towards the forest, and above—the attic with dead flies, secrets and hidden treasure, perhaps even a photo of Ros.

But what happened to the Chinese mugs, so treasured by Mum that we never used them for tea and which I had forgotten all about until I remembered them in a dream? On my way to the loo my eyes fall on a set of shelves by the staircase with coloured glass and various ornaments, and there, right on top, in pride of place, are the two Chinese mugs.

* * *

When I was five years old I was given a book for Christmas that I remember till this day. It was about a little troll-boy living somewhere in the Norwegian mountains. For some reason he decided to venture out into the world of humans, which he did. But he didn't like it here. People were not very nice to him, and he didn't fit in. So, one day he decided to make his way back home. The book had beautiful illustrations, and I remember the final picture: The little troll-boy seen from behind, walking across a mountain plateau ablaze with the colours of autumn, his home somewhere ahead of him, in the distance. The book disappeared and I have no idea what it was called and who wrote it. But, at that early age I think I must have decided to make the troll-boy's story my own.

Party time in the house on the hill, my nephews' wives, Anne Cathrione, Liv, Vibeke, and Yours Truly.

Acknowledgements

This is the story of my father, Kristoffer Hoddevik's, life from a three-year-old in 1905 to old age in the 1970s and early 80s. Some people and events have been disguised. A few names have been changed, but I have endeavoured to stick as closely as possible to the real people and episodes.

For historical facts and background information I have relied on Internet sites such as: Nortraship. Warsailors.com/single ships/herbrand. Nortraship's secret Fund. Arctic Convoys of World War II. Indian Ocean in World War II. Liverpool Blitz. Overthrow of the Shah. National Geographic, Albatross. The Maritime Museum of Liverpool. Local historian Else Fure, Portland Evening Express August 31st 1945. The Norwegian Magazine *Krigsseilieren* (The War-sailor) n. 1 1983. My father's letters, telegrams and diaries 1943 – 45. Stories and anecdotes from the German occupation of Norway told by my mother and others who lived through it. My own memories.

The novels *We, the drowned*, by the Danish author Carsten Jensen, and *Every tenth Man had to die* by the late Norwegian author Per Hanson offered valuable insight into life in the convoys and helped me to recreate the drama and atmosphere of the Battle of the Atlantic.

I want to thank my brother, Karstein, (called John in the book) for rooting about in the attic of our family home digging out old photos, telegrams, newspaper cuttings and my father's wartime diaries. Thanks also to my younger son, Sam, for reading chapters and offering constructive criticism, and to my older son, Adam, for his encouragement and enthusiasm for the project. My thanks go to my friend and colleague Chris Dillon for proof-reading the book twice and offering helpful suggestions and comments, and to his father, the historian Jim Dillon, for valuable historical information, for taking the time to drive me around Liverpool and showing me where my father would have sailed in, anchored and discharged his cargo of oil all those years ago. Thanks also to my friend and former colleague, Dr Martin Stanton, for reading chapters and offering his encouragement. Most of all my thanks to Maher, my dear husband of 42 years, for his encouragement and interest in my father's story, a story that he felt needed to be told, and for his patience when I disappeared into my study for hours on end not wanting to be disturbed. Sadly Maher passed away after a short illness just before the completion of the book.

Made in the USA
Charleston, SC
01 November 2015